DRESSING
DIANA

DRESSING DIANA

TIM GRAHAM
AND
TAMSIN BLANCHARD

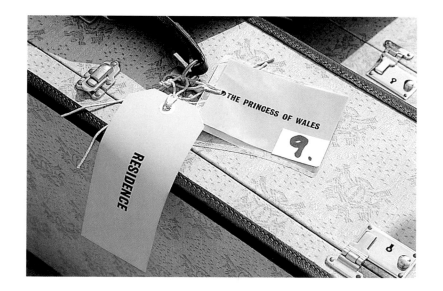

WEIDENFELD & NICOLSON
LONDON

CONTENTS

INTRODUCTION:
THE MAKING OF AN ICON 6

1 **WORKING WARDROBE** 18

2 **A FLAIR FOR COLOUR** 34

3 **DIPLOMATIC DRESSING** 58

4 **A SENSE OF OCCASION** 68

5 **CASUAL CHIC** 102

6 **TRAVELLING WARDROBE** 118

7 **EMERGENCE OF STYLE** 124

8 **THE DESIGNERS** 142

9 **MAKING CHANGES** 182

10 **THE DETAILS** 194

11 **THE LEGACY** 202

CONTENTS **5**

INTRODUCTION

THE MAKING OF AN ICON

ON THE MORNING OF JUNE 26TH, 1997, PRINCESS DIANA RECEIVED A FAX AT KENSINGTON Palace from Christie's auction house in New York. It was the morning after the Dresses sale, one of the most talked about dress auctions in history, which had just raised nearly £2 million for charity by selling off seventy-nine dresses from her collection, adding to the £1.5 million raised from sales of the catalogue alone. In New York the previous evening, the auction house had been filled with a buzz of excitement and apprehension. First to go under the hammer was a three-quarter length sari-inspired silk chiffon evening dress by Gina Fratini for the House of Hartnell. The Princess had worn the romantic dress for a portrait by Patrick Demarchelier and it sold for £51,128. Next under the hammer was the famous Serpentine dress, a sexy black silk cocktail number, worn by the Princess the night of the Prince of Wales's infamous interview with Jonathan Dimblebly on BBC television. The dress had originally been bought off-the-peg for £900. It was a particularly flirty little black dress but, up until the night of the dinner, the name of British-based designer Christina Stambolian had been little known. Here it was however, lot two in the sale of the century and undergoing fierce bidding. Going, going...gone. Sold for £44,511 to Graeme and Briege Mackenzie from Bridge on Weir, Scotland. The designer herself had flown to New York to witness the historic occasion. 'There seems to be some very strange psychology behind the bidding,' she commented to the waiting reporters who formed part of the international media circus that congregated at 502 Park Avenue.

Thirteen of the seventy-nine dresses sold for over £30,000 each, the ink blue silk velvet dinner dress by British couturier Victor Edelstein breaking records and selling for over £133,000. It was not the dress, fabulous as it was, that inspired the frenzy of bidding. It was the magic and romance accompanying the dress that captured the public imagination; when Diana wore it to dance with John Travolta in the ballroom of the White House, the photograph of the event made newspaper front pages. Not only was it Diana's dream to be spun around the dance floor by the star of *Saturday Night Fever* – who was rumoured to have been the secret Californian telephone bidder – it was virtually every other woman's fantasy too. The dress was more than the silk velvet and fine hand stitching that held it together; here was a piece of history and one glorious segment of a romantic fairy tale.

Usually costume auctions are the sole preserve of museums and collectors. The Princess of Wales's sale was different however. Certainly there were representatives from major costume collections alongside private collectors, but what made this auction unique were the crowds of ordinary people who came to watch, to look at the Princess's clothes and indeed to bid themselves. One woman bought a dress that she intended to put on display to fund a stray cats' refuge. A flamenco-inspired red and black dress by Murray Arbeid was bought via telephone bid by British businessman Michael Freedman, who operates a beauty salon that gives clients complete makeovers. His idea was to allow his clients to be photographed in the dress after their makeovers. Two dresses, a short grey silk cocktail dress by Catherine Walker and a stunning fuchsia pink cowl-backed evening dress by Victor Edelstein, were bought by the Fashion Café, to be displayed in New York and London. Another three dresses were bought by American soap channel AMC Romance to be exhibited around America. 'We are a romance channel and Diana represents romance,' said the channel's chief, Kate McEnroe. 'Diana has the sympathy of every woman.' And just to prove it, there was Donna Coffin, who spent £13,835 on a purple crushed velvet evening dress. 'It's not my size and will need major alterations,' she told the swarm of journalists. She bought the dress because, like Diana, she too had married in 1981. She felt that her life was in some way linked with that of the Princess.

THE LEGACY LIVES ON

The most curious purchase of the evening was made by Roxanne Duke of Potomac, Maryland. Ms Duke left the auction house with lot fifty-four draped over her arm after paying over £20,000 for the long-sleeved cream pleated silk dinner dress by Catherine Walker, worn by the Princess at official receptions in London and Nepal. She told a reporter that she intended to remove 200 of the dress's faux pearls to sell as jewellery for charity. 'I don't think pulling off 200 pearls will spoil the dress. There are thousands on it,' she said. Soon afterwards, she wrote to the Princess seeking permission to turn the dress into jewellery. Diana replied, with the best of humour, stating that the dress was now Ms Duke's property and she was free to do with it what she wanted. She was only too glad that the pearls would go to a good cause. In her congratulatory message to Christie's, Diana wrote: 'Words cannot adequately describe my absolute delight at the benefits which the results of this auction will bring to so many people who need succour and support.' The sale, which was originally Prince William's idea, was a phenomenal success and captured the imagination of people around the globe.

THE PARED-DOWN PRINCESS

To publicize the Christie's sale, the Princess posed for leading fashion photographer Mario Testino, to accompany an interview with Cathy Horyn in *Vanity Fair*. Diana wanted to make a clean break with the past, changing her make-up, loosening her hair, and leaving behind the costume jewellery and baubles she liked to wear. This was a new, pared-down Diana and *Vogue's* star photographer did her justice. From the moment the Princess of Wales told him to call her Diana, the photo session couldn't fail. Dappled with natural daylight, her hair a little messy and her make-up clean and fresh, the Princess of Wales made the cover girl of all cover girls. Her eyes shone and her teeth sparkled – the image of the mid-nineties independent woman and as such she made a far more potent image than any fashion model. She was a dynamic woman, thoroughly in tune with the times, wearing for the last time some of her more elegant evening gowns, before they were auctioned to the highest bidder, together with her old life.

Dressing Diana delighted the designers who were entrusted with the privilege as much as it delighted the Princess herself. She was never a slave to fashion, but she enjoyed clothes, evolving a style that revealed her to be a modern classicist. The seventy-nine dresses sold at auction were all by British designers she patronized over the years, and chief among them was Catherine Walker of the Chelsea Design Company, the designer whose work evolved with Diana's own style from the first year of her marriage to the later years as a chic and stylish independent mother and working woman. Catherine Walker was born in Aix-en-Provence in France and moved to Britain in the seventies after reading philosophy at Lille University. She taught herself to sew and make dresses after her husband died in a tragic accident in 1975. She learned how to make tailored clothes for children out of necessity – she had two baby daughters to support – and as therapy to deal with her grief. She sold the clothes 'like a gypsy, out of a basket on the King's Road' and eventually built on her success by buying premises. By 1988,

Catherine Walker was able to concentrate on couture clothing, each design made by hand and to fit each individual customer. Her talent was duly rewarded, and before the decade was out she had become firmly established as a designer of choice to the rich and famous as well as a network of royals, from Queen Noor of Jordan to the Duchess of Kent. With Princess Diana Walker established a unique and special bond that verged on the telepathic.

Part of the secret of Diana's successful partnership with Catherine Walker was the designer's discretion and her intuitive understanding of the Princess's sartorial needs. She worked on a system of dressing that formed the backbone of Diana's official working wardrobe, often in tandem with hat or shoe designers, sending sketches and fabric swatches to milliner Philip Somerville or shoe designer Jimmy Choo, who would accessorize the dress or suit immaculately. While Walker would never have used her relationship with the Princess as a PR exercise, Diana invited the designer and her team of *petits mains*, the people who cut, sew, tailor and embroider for the house, to pose with her for a special picture by Tim Graham reproduced in this book. For a morning, Kensington Palace was transformed into a couturier's *atelier*, with the designer, her staff and some of the dresses that were to be sold at Christie's on show on mannequins.

THE MAKING OF A FAIRY PRINCESS

At the beginning of her public career, the young Lady Diana Spencer was introduced to the fashion house Bellville Sassoon, a discreet little salon just off the King's Road in the heart of Chelsea. Belinda Bellville has since retired, but David Sassoon remains the designer, now in partnership with Lorcan Mullany. He has probably dressed more Royals than any other designer, from his first royal commission for the ten-year-old Princess Anne in 1960 when she was a bridesmaid for Lord Mountbatten's daughter Pamela, to Princess Margaret, Princess Alexandra, Princess Michael of Kent, and most famously, Princess Diana. She was first taken to Bellville Sassoon by her mother Frances Shand-Kydd, a long-established client of the designer. In turn, Diana later introduces the young Lady Sarah Armstrong-Jones, daughter of Princess Margaret and Lord Snowdon, to David Sassoon, buying Lady Sarah's first evening dress as a present.

David Sassoon made some of Diana's most princess-like dresses of that early period. One of Diana's favourites was the Gonzaga dress, worn to the opening of the *Splendours of the Gonzagas* exhibition at the Victoria and Albert museum, the night before the Palace announced that she was expecting a baby, when her lowered head made the press report that she had fallen asleep.

'It was a fairy princess dress with a big skirt, very pretty,' says Sassoon, fondly remembering the early days when Diana's style was at its most naive. Not everything was a success in those days. One dress worn to the State opening of Parliament was, says Sassoon, 'not one I was greatly fond of. It was the Princess's idea of conforming to Royal dressing.' Sassoon has kept all the books filled with sketches and designs sent out to Diana for her approval, a very personal form of home shopping. She would return the books with hand-written notes on the pages: 'This in dark blue, please,' or simply, 'Yes, please,' would mark her orders.

INDEPENDENT WOMAN

David Sassoon witnessed the change in Diana from Sloane Ranger into Princess and then during the early nineties into independent woman. 'As soon as she was no longer married, she changed. She knew she could dress for herself,' he comments. The last dress commissioned from Bellville Sassoon was a simple elegant long black draped dress with a bow at the side of the waist and embroidered chains as straps. She wore it to a premiere of the Kirov Ballet's *Romeo and Juliet*. 'It was very different from the earlier dresses,' says Sassoon. 'By then she had very definite ideas of how she liked to dress. I did notice a tremendous change.' The dress was sold at auction for almost £14,000. 'Once she became an independent woman, she didn't have to wear English clothes – she could spread her wings. It gave a completely different slant to her style.'

The different slant came in the form of the late Gianni Versace. What Versace did for Diana was what he did for all his customers: he gave her sex appeal and a strongly modern style. During the eighties, he was nicknamed the King of Glitz and he epitomized flashy Italian dressing, with garish baroque prints, gilt geegaws and collections inspired by bondage and brothels. But as the nineties unfolded, Versace discovered minimalism and stripped down his designs to make plain pastel-coloured suits with discreet little buttons and dresses that dazzled with their daring cutting rather than their brightly coloured prints. The timing was perfect and the new look Versace suited Diana admirably. She had the ideal body shape for his clothes – tall and leggy at five foot ten, athletically slim, her measurements 36–26–36, a dress size 12. When Diana wanted to become better known for her work than for her wardrobe, fashion's new understatement could not have been better timed. Gone was the fairy-tale princess, and in came a more realistic image of working mother, a woman in control of her own destiny. Versace's designs proved a to be a turning point in her own personal style.

It was typical of Diana to wear an Italian designer's dress to meet Pavarotti at a performance in Italy in September 1995. Versace fitted the bill and she wore a specially commissioned white silk crêpe dress with a low decolletage and diamanté buckles. She had worn a similar design in black the previous week, to attend a movie premiere. Although she would never have gone so far as the dramatic dress barely secured by safety pins worn by Elizabeth Hurley, the evening gowns she wore by Versace, as well as the cocktail dresses and the tailored suits, held her in, pushed her up and gave her length – and curves – in all the right places. A Versace gown is deceptively simple. Inside, there is a clever system of boning and underpinning to give shape, curves and structure to the wearer. The designer knew how to make the most of a woman's assets, and whenever Diana wore Versace, the next day's tabloids would have little choice but to comment on her impressive cleavage. One of the most striking of Versace's dresses for the Princess was a precision-cut purple dress made for a dinner in Chicago in 1996. This time there was no cleavage, just a clever shaped neckline with a tiny V-shape cut into the front, and armholes cut to show off those athletic shoulders. Diana chose to accessorize the look with amethyst jewellery and a bag and shoes made by Jimmy Choo to match the colour of the dress exactly. Earlier in the day, she had worn one of the designer's neatly tailored demure suits for a visit to Cook County Hospital.

STYLE ICON

In February 1997, Diana agreed to endorse a fund-raising book for Versace called *Rock and Royalty* with a signed foreword. However, the charity gala at which Diana was to be guest of honour was cancelled at the last minute when the Princess deemed pictures of the Royal Family interspersed with Versace's own imagery – a mixture of supermodels and nudes – to be inappropriate. The money that would have been spent on the party was sent to an AIDS charity. After his murder in Miami in July 1997, Princess Diana attended Gianni Versace's funeral and gave support to other mourners, including her friend Elton John with whom she had fallen out over the *Rock and Royalty* incident. 'I am devastated by the loss of a great and talented man,' she said of Versace, who had by then become one of her favourite designers.

By 1995 Diana's transformation from Shy Di of the British tabloids to Princess of Fashion was complete. She was invited by Liz Tilberis, the editor of *Harper's Bazaar*, to present a prize at the Council of Fashion Designers of America Awards in New York. To the delight of Tilberis, the

Princess accepted the invitation and the New York fashion fraternity embraced Diana with open arms. She was every fashionable party's most wanted guest. But her most important fashion moment was still to come. The following year Diana was the guest of honour at the Costume Institute on the New York Metropolitan Museum's annual gala night. The evening opened the museum's fifty-year retrospective of Christian Dior. The Princess made her entrance in a dress that will go down in the annals of fashion history: the first gown to be designed for Dior by the new and controversial British designer-in-chief, John Galliano, who had just taken over the position from Italian couturier Gianfranco Ferré. The dress and Galliano were given an official inauguration before the world's press, after several fittings at Kensington Palace, including one on the morning of John Galliano's birthday when the Princess organized a champagne breakfast for him. The day after the gala, newspapers everywhere carried a picture of the Princess of Wales in the midnight blue satin crêpe, lingerie-inspired evening dress, edged in black lace and with a train at the back. As usual, the comments were not all complimentary. One British tabloid said the Princess looked as though she had gone sleepwalking in her nightie. But for the House of Dior, all publicity was good publicity, especially when its name and that of Diana's were linked in the same picture caption. It was an unprecedented publicity coup.

CLOSE SCRUTINY

Since the day her engagement was announced Diana became accustomed to seeing her picture splashed across the world's newspapers. It was not just newspaper editors who were fascinated by her; the public appetite for images of her seemed insatiable. They would follow avidly every change of hairstyle, shade of eyeliner and shape of neckline. When she so much as moved the parting of her hair, it was seen as a matter of national significance. At times, the superficiality irritated the Princess, especially when causes that she campaigned for were ignored in favour of a few column inches on the length of her skirts. Diana did learn to some extent how to work with the press, and to manipulate them as much as they tried to manipulate her. She was aware that her image could sell tens of thousands of newspapers or magazines and knew exactly what to wear if she wanted to make headlines. The problem was there was little she could wear that wouldn't make headlines. Diana had also learned early on in her public career about the language of clothes and the power they could have. She was always conscious of dressing appropriately and learned quickly from her mistakes.

In 1992, when her marriage was on the verge of collapse, Diana chose to tell the world by posing alone in front of the Taj Mahal. The Catherine Walker outfit she wore for the occasion was a newspaper picture editor's dream, a guaranteed front page hit. She chose a vivid red bolero, violet knee-length skirt and butter silk blouse, an outfit she had recycled by cutting a few inches off the hem of the skirt since its first appearance in Hong Kong in 1989. It was a postcard home to her fans in vivid Technicolour. The red of her jacket stood out from the sparkling white of the Taj Mahal and the bright azure blue of the sky like the St George cross in the Union Jack.

GETTING THE MESSAGE ACROSS

Two years later in 1994 Diana was to make her point through her dress again on the night Jonathan Dimbleby's interview with the Prince of Wales was broadcast on television. Diana looked dazzling in an off-the-peg black ruched slip of a cocktail dress by Christina Stambolian as she emerged from her limousine to greet the world's press outside the Serpentine Gallery. She wanted the world to know she was just fine without the Prince and would continue her life unabashed. By any standards, it was a wonderfully sexy, party-girl dress. Cleverly, Diana chose to set it off with her trademark pearl and sapphire choker; the piece of jewellery, along with her engagement ring, that most symbolized her role as Princess of Wales and mother of the future King of England. She looked fresh, sophisticated, modern and ebullient. The press of course went wild. Once again Charles was upstaged by his wife.

The contrast between Diana's own television interview with *Panorama's* Martin Bashir in November 1995 and her first broadcast alongside her fiancé in 1981 tells the whole story. In 1981, the young nineteen-year-old wore a outfit in which the Queen herself would not have looked out of place. She hid her eyes under her heavy fringe, looking shy and intimidated. Fourteen years on, rather than hide them, the Princess drew attention to her eyes by outlining them in black smudgy kohl and mascara. In place of the sensible mumsy print outfit was a business-like jacket and plain white silk top. She wanted to look strong and assertive, keeping the viewers' attention focused on what she was saying rather than what she was wearing.

Similarly, Diana was able to draw attention to her good works by dressing the part in the minefields of Angola. She had no choice but to don the bullet-proof vest and helmet, while the khaki pants and sleeveless chambray shirts were proof that she was working and getting her hands dirty. The sunny clothes she wore on her charity visits were a manifestation of the famous

Diana human touch. When visiting AIDS patients or sick children, she would wear something bright and cheery, literally bringing a breath of fresh air with her as she entered a room. It was this sensibility that lent Diana her popular appeal. Sshe felt very strongly that she was dressing for her public and would never let them down.

TRUSTED ADVISORS

Throughout her public career, Diana was not without knowledgeable advisors. In the early days she was introduced to Anna Harvey, deputy editor of British *Vogue*, who helped her through many a sartorial quandary from her engagement onwards. Through Harvey, she met Liz Tilberis, then a fashion editor but later editor of British *Vogue* who moved to New York to edit *Harper's Bazaar*, remaining a close friend. *Vogue* helped mould Diana's fashionable image over the years, from her first sitting for the magazine at the age of nineteen with Lord Snowdon in 1981 when she wore virginal white lace, to the birthday portraits by Patrick Demarchelier on the cover of *Vogue* in July 1994 when she was thirty-three. 'She wanted to be modern rather than fashionable,' recalled Anna Harvey in her tribute to Diana in the issue of *Vogue* following the tragedy of her sudden death. 'After the divorce she was much freer,' noted Harvey. 'She wore a lot of Versace – the simple shift dresses and evening columns that he and Catherine Walker were doing for her this past year were probably her most successful look to date.' Anna Harvey's own clean, easy style was a great influence on Diana, who looked to her for guidance and advice, although she did not always take it. She was always her own woman, listening to advice, but following her own instincts.

Through Anna Harvey as well as through her own personal exploration, Diana met many British designers, both young and more established, as well as the hair and make-up team, Sam McKnight and Mary Greenwell, who were booked for a *Vogue* sitting in 1990 and continued a long-standing relationship with her. There were the Emanuels who made, among other creations, the most copied wedding dress in history; Bruce Oldfield whom she met a few weeks after her wedding and who designed some of the Princess's most glamorous evening dresses of the eighties; Jasper Conran, Roland Klein, Caroline Charles, Edina Ronay, Rifat Ozbek, twice winner of the British Fashion Designer of the Year Award, Amanda Wakeley, Tomasz Starzewski and Murray Arbeid were just some of the designers who contributed to the Princess's wardrobe as she shopped around, experimenting with clothes for endless official functions, tours and state occasions. One of her favourites was the couturier, Victor Edelstein whose made-to-measure, hand-stitched clothes started at around £1,800 for a day dress and rose steeply from £3,000 for evening wear; ten of his dresses for Diana were sold at the Christie's auction.

Edelstein worked at Alexon, at Biba for Barbara Hulanicki and Christian Dior London before starting out on his own in 1977. He began to make couture in 1981 after his ready-to-wear business went into liquidation. An evening dress made completely by hand would take at least three weeks and he made about six dresses a year for the Princess over a period of ten years. He gave up couture in the early nineties for a quieter, less stressful life as a painter living between Andalusia and Venice. Diana would attend one of Edelstein's twice-yearly couture shows in London; or he would show her clothes. Fittings were usually done at Kensington Palace. 'She was clear about her likes and dislikes,' he told *Hello!* magazine the month before the Christie's auction. 'She would choose a certain dress and ask me which other colours it was made in. It was a collaboration like any other between designer and client...she had a good eye for what would suit her.' Edelstein's dresses for Diana were always clean and elegant. He was as much a technician as an artist and knew how to cut a dress to flatter a woman. When Diana commissioned him to make an ink blue silk velvet dinner dress to wear in America, it was not until he saw the pictures the next day that he discovered it was worn to the White House. But it was not such a surprise. He knew and she knew that it looked stunning, as did the oyster duchesse satin bolero and dinner dress embroidered and beaded with pearls, carnations and birds that Diana wore to a State banquet with President and Madame Mitterrand in Paris in 1988; a dress she could hardly bear to part with for the auction.

DRESSING HER AGE

One mark of the Princess's emerging confidence and independence was her ever-decreasing skirt lengths. On a trip to Venice in June 1995, the hems that had been creeping upwards above her knees reached daring heights in the form of a sparkly red georgette dress by Casablanca-born Knightsbridge-based designer, Jacques Azagury. Up until the early nineties, Diana's skirts were kept firmly below the knee. As she began to dress her age, a youthful thirty-something, Diana began to show off her legs. 'She probably had the most fantastic legs I have ever seen. The best legs,' enthused Azagury who made around eighteen dresses for Diana. He tried to encourage her to go just that little bit shorter. 'In the last eighteen months to two years of her life, the Princess

LEFT TO RIGHT
Diana attended the
London gala for the
Dresses sale at
Christie's wearing a
Catherine Walker
shift. Beside her is the
pale pink and white
off-the-shoulder dress
by Catherine Walker
that she wore to the
Royal Ballet in Berlin
1987 (far right).

changed her look a lot,' he says. 'She was not quite so grown up or princessy any more. After her divorce, she knew she didn't have to live by the rules. She was starting to wear things she may have wanted to wear for some time. Her wardrobe became seriously international – young, sexy, slinky and everything to do with fashion.' Indeed, the contrast between the first Jacques Azagury dress with its modest flapper-style skirt that the Princess wore while in Florence in 1985, and the red dress worn in Venice with its very short hem in 1995 was marked. She had seen the first dress on his stand when she visited the London Designer Exhibition, and was transfixed the moment she saw the black and blue ballerina-length dress with shiny blue stars embroidered on the rayon velvet sprinkled with glitter. This dress was the only Azagury gown to go into the Dresses sale, perhaps because his recent designs were generally more modern and functional and would continue to be useful.

Diana would sometimes choose dresses from the rails in Azagury's Knightsbridge boutique. 'She enjoyed coming into the shop,' he recalls. Indeed, she enjoyed shopping generally. 'Since Princess Margaret in the sixties, there had never been a show person in the monarchy for British fashion. And then this young girl came along and brightened up the Royal Family. She loved dressing up and got very excited about trying on new designs.' Azagury considered it a great privilege that he had the chance to dress Diana, maintaining, 'She was the perfect woman to dress, and totally unique. She could give any supermodel or actress a run for her money.'

By the mid-nineties, Diana had indeed become her own woman, intent on living her life as she wanted to. Her divorce behind her, she was concentrating on her most heartfelt charity work as well as bringing up her children. It was not what she wore that was important and she made it known that although she enjoyed clothes, her work meant far more to her than what she was wearing. As with all the world's best-dressed women, it was not what she wore but the way she wore it that was really important – she looked as stylish in a pair of jeans with her shirt sleeves rolled up, as she did in a couture ball gown. Ultimately, her style transcended her clothes and had much more to do with the twinkle in her eye and that smile that made everyone who knew her or who came into her life feel at ease. Designer names can be bought, but taste and style are priceless. Diana, Princess of Wales was blessed more than most with those attributes.

BELOW Diana signs a catalogue at the New York party before the Christie's sale. She wore a champagne-coloured Catherine Walker shift similar to that worn at the London party.

WORKING WARDROBE

*T*HE WORKING WARDROBE OF THE PRINCESS OF WALES took in its stride ceremonial pomp and circumstance, royal regalia, clothes for walkabouts in the heat of the Australian sun or a visit to Wales on a rainy, windswept afternoon, as well as outfits for state occasions in England and abroad, a day at the races, or visiting the sick and dying. For most women, a working wardrobe is a mere matter of a few business suits and matching shoes, and the odd long dress to be hauled from the back of the wardrobe once a year for an evening event. For the Princess of Wales, the building up of a working wardrobe was a full time job in itself. She had unique and ever-changing needs.

There are few positions that require four or five changes of dress a day. The whole point of late twentieth-century fashion is that women can wear the same outfit from morning through to evening with the addition perhaps of jewellery, but no actual change of dress. But Diana was living a life of formality and protocol that had not changed for hundreds of years — a life that required a day dress, an afternoon dress and a separate dress code for theatre, dinner, charity functions or a gala ball. Diana had to plan her wardrobe around the varied appointments and functions of her day, and she also had to contend with the

LEFT TO RIGHT
Diana visited the British
Lung Foundation in a
pale blue bouclé suit by
Chanel from their 1997
spring/summer
collection. The details –
fringed lapels, inset
pocket detailing, slim
above-the-knee skirt and
high heels – added to
her projected image as a
polished, sophisticated
and serious professional
woman of the nineties.

ABOVE A departure
from the usual neat
clutch bag, this beige
handbag completes
the chic outfit.

continual gaze of cameras, dissecting her every move and every fashion choice she made. Nothing was above scrutiny; her hairstyles, make-up and jewellery all commanded attention.

GETTING IT RIGHT

A key to Diana's style was her versatility and ability to get it right – to wear waterproofs on board a naval ship, gold braid and frogging to a military parade, or a soft floral dress and matching hat on a walkabout with her husband, and always to look like she was in the right place at the right time in the right outfit. She played several different roles at once and dressed the part perfectly, but it was not always easy. The weather, for one thing, was an unreliable factor that could destroy an outfit or plumed hat with a single downpour. Even in the rain the Princess managed to look unselfconscious and radiant.

For the first part of her working life, Diana served mainly as a figurehead for charities. After her divorce, she concentrated on fewer charities and devoted more time and energy to each one. She became both figurehead and another pair of hard-working hands. With her shirt sleeves rolled up, she was ready for first-hand experience rather than charity fund-raising alone. Her wardrobe became less oriented towards big dresses for big dinners and more to khaki jeans, chambray shirts and functional clothes for expeditions that were to include a high profile journey to the mine fields of Angola for the Red Cross and the Halo Trust, and a visit to landmine victims in Bosnia.

Diana wore a pale pink tailored suit to an awards luncheon at the Savoy in March 1997. The suit, by Catherine Walker, has three-quarter length sleeves with cuffs that echo the design of the collar. Also note the simplicity of the pearl earrings and the bag by Versace. Catherine Walker was the designer who most clearly understood the requirements of Diana's public wardrobe, designing many of the outfits that Diana wore throughout her sixteen years of public life.

LEFT AND BELOW A close-up of the classic Chanel court shoe typical of Diana's later, sleeker style. The Princess wore this business-like Versace suit (*below*) to a landmine campaign press briefing held in Washington in June, 1997.

D URING THE YEARS OF HER MARRIAGE, PRINCESS DIANA didn't wear high heels because she did not want to tower over her husband who, at five feet ten, was the same height. She only needed an extra two inches to take her to a towering six feet. She wore plain, low-heeled shoes during the eighties and patronized names such as Charles Jourdan, Clive Shilton and Alexander Gabbay of Ivory. She had dozens of pairs of shoes from Rayne and Gina, specifically matched to particular outfits. But as the nineties progressed Diana's heels got higher. She wore shoes by Manolo Blahnik, as well as ordering from designer Jimmy Choo, whose flat shoes and wonderful strappy high heels were part of her more recent look. She also wore a classic, heeled court shoe, often with contrasting toe. When Diana called Jimmy Choo to make her a pair of shoes to wear to the party to launch her dress sale at Christie's, she chose a very slim and very high shoe. Choo told her they would be difficult to walk in with their three-and-three-quarter-inch heels, but she was undeterred, knowing that she would be getting out of a limousine and wouldn't have to walk very far. If a princess can't wear high heels, nobody can. The heels could also have been construed as a symbol of confidence and the beginning of a new and happier life.

PINSTRIPE VARIATIONS

LEFT TO RIGHT
Pinstripes were an important part of Diana's working wardrobe, as designed here by Catherine Walker. She used stripes for suits, jackets and dresses; sometimes combining a dress and jacket for a more feminine twist to the traditional city fabric. A business-like jacket and skirt (*left*) worn after the divorce in 1994; a cream and black suit worn in 1991 (*centre*) and a snappy pinstripe dress (*right*) for an RAF visit the same year, both of satinized wool.

The Princess of Wales in Germany as Colonel-in-Chief of the Light Dragoons. She was always conscious of dressing for her different roles and on this occasion chose navy and white to echo the soldiers' uniforms. The fine silk suit with a white leather belt, and white collar and cuffs is by Catherine Walker. The hat by Philip Somerville has a white silk gazaar crown and drape with a bow at the side, the synamay boater brim is edged in white.

RIGHT AND BELOW Philip Somerville's turban hat and matching Escada coat (*right*), designed for a trip to Berlin, but worn here boarding a ship on the Isle of Wight in November, 1987. Diana added her own belt to the coat. She stepped out of an Australian bus (*below*) in a Victor Edelstein dress and hat by Frederick Fox, 1985.

RIGHT Diana wore this navy and white suit for the commemoration of the Battle of the Atlantic. She carried her briefcase down the steps at Heathrow airport on her way back from Liverpool. In her other hand is a hat by Philip Somerville that matched the navy and white nautical outfit by Catherine Walker.

LEFT Diana's red and black military-style coat, with its double row of black buttons, by Piero de Monzi, matches the Lord Lieutenant's uniform. She was conscious of dressing for her public and often wore bright colours to stand out in a crowd. Marina Killery made the black velvet-crowned hat with a 'V 'split back in 1984; in 1986, while going through a Cossack-look phase, Diana had a muff made to match the stylish hat.

LEFT Coats were a difficult part of the working wardrobe to get right, but were necessary for cold winter walkabouts. This cream cashmere and wool coat trimmed with fake beaver by Arabella Pollen, kept the Princess warm as she met the people of Hamburg in 1987. The fake fur fabric floppy beret is by Gilly Forge.

ABOVE AND RIGHT Diana took into account not just the event but the place too. She wore this jade green coat by the Emanuels to visit Venice in May 1985. The hat, also by the Emanuels, with its unusual upturned brim echoes the collar of the coat.

2

A FLAIR FOR COLOUR

THE PRINCESS WAS NOT AFRAID OF COLOUR, AND OVER the years she wore the full spectrum. The colours she wore again and again were vivid pillar-box red, royal blue, classic navy and white, sugar-plum fairy pink and ice blue. She often chose the colour of her outfit to fit the occasion – a military parade might mean a snappy navy and white outfit, or one in royal blue. She also loved to wear black, feeling it was chic and sophisticated but, as she found out when she wore a black taffeta dress by the Emanuels soon after her engagement, the colour has a special place in the protocol of Royal dressing, and is usually reserved for funerals and mourning. Diana was not afraid of the colour and had a number of day dresses, suits and evening wear in black. It was a colour that suited her.

The wardrobe of the later, more pared-down Diana contained a palette of pastel shades and neutral beiges for both night and day. She stopped trying to colour co-ordinate every outfit and would wear beige shoes, a black bag and a pale green suit with more confidence than when she once wore monochrome red or green from head to foot. Her use of colour became more low key and subtle.

Her sometimes skewed sense of colour – most women would balk at the thought of a canary yellow dress, or a bright orange suit, but not Diana – often worked surprisingly well. When a Catherine Walker coat dress in pink and red was presented to the milliner Philip Somerville, he said, 'The Princess put colours together that even I was surprised by, like pink and red, or green and blue.'

GREAT
GREENS

LEFT AND RIGHT
Princess Diana liked
to experiment with
colours and would
often dress from head
to toe in the same
shade. The green
Catherine Walker suit
(*left*), with its double
row of buttons and
matching court shoes,
was worn on a trip to
Korea in 1992. The
green snug-fitting
tailored suit with
black velvet collar
detailing, by Victor
Edelstein (*right*), was
worn during a visit
to Lisbon in
February 1987.

SHADES
OF BLUE

LEFT Diana would dress all in one colour (*far left*) or break it up with a print hat (*left*), or wear a blue suit with a white silk blouse (*below left*). The blue and white print hat, by Graham Smith at Kangol, matches the blouse worn with this swing-back Catherine Walker suit.

RIGHT During a trip to Austria, Diana spotted this wool flannel, black polka dot seven-eighths length coat and matching silk satin blouse with flock spots, by designer Jan Vanvelden in a fashion show and ordered it for her Canadian tour in May 1986. He had only three weeks to make it. The hat in cobalt blue satin, like the one opposite, was designed by Graham Smith at Kangol.

LEFT When Diana liked a colour, she sometimes overdid it and co-ordinated everything to match, from her hat down to her tights. For this visit to Cirencester in February 1985, she decided not to wear red shoes to match the red Jan Vanvelden suit.

ABOVE This red and white print dress with lace insert and bow was worn on several occasions, including to polo matches and while on a tour to Thailand in 1988.

LEFT Just a hint of polka dot at the neck and wrist of this belted red suit worn to Suffolk Agricultural Association County Show in May 1986. Note the small shoulder bag in exactly the same shade of red.

ABOVE A red and white sailor-style contrast jacket was worn over a silk polka dot dress by Catherine Walker in both Australia and Canada. The brimmed hat by John Boyd was essential in the Australian sun.

LEFT A close-up
detail of a finely
crafted jacket cuff and
patent leather clutch
bag – the straight skirt
and black tights
complete the look.
Catherine Walker
knew intuitively how
to dress Diana, down
to the last detail.

LEFT By 1989 Diana had refined the art of wearing colour, and wore this curvy red jacket by Catherine Walker with a svelte black dress to great effect. Vines and grapes embroidered around the front of the jacket take the place of a collar and lapels, and on the pockets in place of flaps. The simple curve of the jacket is very figure flattering.

LEFT Diana bought this off-the-peg tartan jacket the afternoon she was due to switch on the Christmas lights in 1993. 'She often did things in such a rush,' says David Sassoon. That afternoon, Diana had visited Bellville Sassoon's Chelsea shop, saw the jacket and was wearing it just a few hours later.

ABOVE Diana wore this tartan outfit by Caroline Charles with a bow blouse. The designer had made two tartan suits for Diana to wear to the Braemar Games in Scotland. Puff sleeves and big hair hint at an early move towards the later Dynasty look.

RIGHT A tartan coat dress with bright red accents by Catherine Walker worn on a visit to Japan in 1990. The traditional tartan was given a very modern, clean shape. Later this coat was given an updated look by shortening the hem to sit above the knee.

LEFT Diana had an instinct for mixing unexpected colours and making them work. This pink and red hat by Philip Somerville is one of his favourite designs for the Princess, made to match the coat dress by Catherine Walker. The clean cut and bright colours were a hit when the Princess arrived in Dubai in March 1989. The dress was later shortened and appeared again in Egypt in 1992.

ABOVE Few women can get away with bright orange, but Diana could with this belted Versace suit worn with the famous Dior Diana handbag, opaque lycra tights and polo jumper for extra warmth.

RIGHT A deep turquoise Catherine Walker jacket made for a wedding. The cross-over style with decorative buttons was one the designer successfully repeated again and again for Diana.

Red and white was always a good colour combination for the Garter Ceremony, blending perfectly with the red of the Guards' jackets. The elaborate white lace Puritan collared blouse by Jan Vanvelden was a favourite of Diana's and was typical of her style in 1985. Jan Vanvelden designed mostly day clothes for the Princess and once remarked 'She's wonderful to work with because she is interested in what you are doing.'

RIGHT Diana always dressed appropriately for State and ceremonial occasions. At the Garter Ceremony at Windsor in 1986, she wore a black and white coat dress by Catherine Walker to echo Charles' robes. The ruffle down one side of the neckline softens the line, and her hat, bag and shoes are two-tone to match the dress.

RIGHT Diana wore a navy and white suit by society dressmaker Tomasz Starzewski for the VJ Day parade in 1995. The hat, of white synamay straw with a flared crown and a small brim trimmed with navy satin, by Philip Somerville matched the piped detail of the suit. Note the pearl earrings to match the single strand of pearls and her sapphire engagement ring.

BLACK AND WHITE

LEFT A white suit is given shape by a wide black waist cincher. Sheer black tights, black bag and high-heel shoes complete the ensemble worn to open a new London centre for HIV and AIDS patients at the end of 1994. Diana had black and navy versions of this bag by Ferragamo.

RIGHT This was a popular design by Catherine Walker for the Princess, made here in black and white dogtooth check, and worn to the Marchioness disaster memorial service in 1989. It is similar to the red and pink dress worn by the Princess in Dubai.

RIGHT The short sleeves of this cream raw silk suit are finely detailed with satin embroidery and scalloped edges. Diana wore pearl earrings to match the buttons and a two-tone Marina Killery hat to the Gulf Forces Parade in June 1991.

PASTEL
BLUES

RIGHT By the nineties, Diana was used to wearing a more natural shoulder line and she favoured more subtle, pastel colours, particularly ice blue and pale pink. Pastels were also a favourite of Versace at this time, who made this pale blue, short-skirted, high-buttoning suit.

LEFT A pale eau de nil suit by Catherine Walker with classic Chanel sling-back shoes and Chanel bag. Diana wore her pearl choker with this pared-down collarless jacket in Chicago, June 1996.

LEFT The duck egg blue coat dress is almost as softly tailored as a cardigan with its rounded shoulders. By the mid-nineties, Diana was wearing her hems above the knee and her heels very high; the strappy shoes worn here are by Gina. The pastel shades she favoured in the latter years highlighted her golden tan.

PRETTY PINKS

LEFT AND ABOVE

Diana wore this pink Jackie O-style, short sleeve jacket and skirt by Versace to Argentina in 1995. Note the clever slit seam detail at the hem of the skirt. The bag is Christian Dior.

ABOVE A polka dot skirt and pink jacket by Paul Costelloe is teamed with matching courts and bag for a trip to Nepal in 1993.

RIGHT Diana looked her best in tailored clothes, and Catherine Walker knew how to structure a jacket. This flirty, swing-style long jacket was worn in Paris, with a bag by Ferragamo.

RIGHT AND BELOW The Princess often chose sandy colours for visits to desert countries. This dupion dress was designed for Diana specifically with Egypt and hot weather in mind.

RIGHT The crisp
cream collar and
tailored detailing
highlight the
practicality of this
tan-coloured dress by
Catherine Walker.
The sleeves cover the
elbow and the hem
was over the knee, to
accord with Middle
Eastern sensibilities
on this Egyptian tour.
Diana teamed it with
flat, sensible two-tone
shoes for walking on
stony ground.

3

DIPLOMATIC DRESSING

*A*S WELL AS DRESSING FOR HER PUBLIC, THE Princess of Wales proved herself adept at dressing the role of the diplomat. She made it known that she saw her role in life as an ambassador for Britain, and she certainly proved that she knew how to dress diplomatically. She developed a finely tuned sense of the right clothes for the occasion and place. She and her designers took into consideration the culture and customs of a particular country she was to visit and planned accordingly. She would wear an Escada coat to visit Germany, a Yuki dress to meet the Japanese Emperor Hirohito, or a Chanel suit to Paris. In Asia and the Middle East, where dress codes for women are strict, Diana demonstrated her sensitivity to local customs while maintaining her personal style. When not 'going native' in a *shalwar kameez*, as she did on several occasions when visiting India or Pakistan, Diana would dress with respect or wit to fit in with the accepted dress code of the particular country. She chose colours to complement national flags – her red and white Rising Sun ensemble delighted the Japanese people and provided the perfect picture opportunity too. For her 1989 Gulf tour, the Princess made sure that her skirts were to the calf or longer, and that her chest and arms were

For her Gulf tour in November 1986 Diana chose this off-the-peg jacket and pleated skirt combination by Jacques Azagury. The Princess usually wore evening dresses by Azagury, but chose this skirt for its length and the jacket because it was so modestly cut. The hat, by Philip Somerville, has a white paribuntal Breton brim with a trimmed white silk band.

OUTDOOR BANQUET SAUDI-STYLE

covered. In Saudi Arabia, Diana was as discreet as an unveiled woman can be, but it was not until a desert picnic that Diana wore the *piece de resistance* of the trip – a long blue and white print silk tunic worn over white silk trousers made by Catherine Walker. Along with Jemima Khan, Diana made the *shalwar kameez* a high society must-have in fashionable western wardrobes. Both women wore hand-crafted *shalwar kameez* from Ritu Kenar, the society dressmaker who has dominated the Indian fashion scene for twenty years and who specializes in luxurious fabrics and the *haute couture* of traditional Indian dress.

LEFT Diana was a true diplomat when it came to fashion. For the desert picnic in Al-Ain she chose a light, airy, blue and white print tunic worn over pyjama-style pants by Catherine Walker. She knew she looked the part as she smiled for Tim Graham's candid picture in March 1989. During the visit, Diana was given a pair of crescent-shaped earrings as a gift.

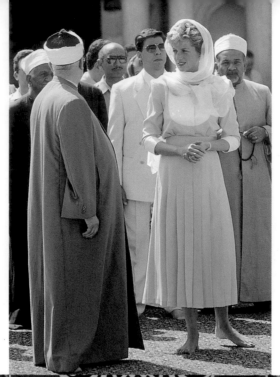

ABOVE AND RIGHT
When Diana entered the
mosque, she removed her
shoes and covered her hair
with a chiffon scarf in
accordance with Muslim
custom, still letting her fringe
peek through at the front.

LEFT A modest day dress by Catherine Walker was perfect for a visit to the Al-Azhar Mosque, Cairo, in May 1992. The dress was first worn on a visit to Nigeria and reflects the colours of the Nigerian flag.

O̶N A VISIT TO THE AL-AZHAR MOSQUE IN CAIRO, Princess Diana wore a pale green bib-front dress by Catherine Walker, buttoned high to the neck, with three-quarter length sleeves and a skirt to her calves. In accordance with Muslim custom, she was required to cover her hair and she came prepared with a chiffon scarf which she wrapped around her head loosely, like a 1950s Grace Kelly. Seven years earlier, when she had met the Pope in Rome, Diana covered her hair in the name of decorum with a black lace veil that matched the back-buttoned black lace Catherine Walker dress made specially for the visit.

In Japan, the Princess paid tribute to Japanese design in a one-off creation by the London-based Japanese designer Yuki. For the same trip, Diana had found a red and white polka dot day dress in a Fulham Road boutique that playfully echoed the Japanese flag. She carried this motif further by teaming the dress with a hat designed by Frederick Fox which echoed the Rising Sun national flag. It was done tastefully, with the crown of the hat forming a round red dot, a lovely tribute to the Emperor. When Diana was presented with a kimono, she did not just accept the gift, she insisted on putting it on over the top of her own dress there and then.

RIGHT Diana was presented with a traditional cotton kimono on her trip to Japan in 1986 and tried it on immediately over her polka dot dress, a strange combination of east meets west. As always, the Princess displayed a healthy sense of humour during the proceedings which endeared her to the people she met.

RIGHT Diana found this polka dot dress in Tatters and bought it specifically for her trip to Japan. She had bought several dresses over the years from the Fulham Road boutique, including some maternity wear and a ball gown. Frederick Fox made a Rising Sun hat to match both the dress and the Japanese flag for the visit. Her witty and thoughtful choice was not lost on the Japanese people and won her many fans.

LEFT Catherine Walker designed this calf-length black lace dress for Diana's audience with the Pope in April 1985. The back view reveals the exquisite button detailing. Protocol demanded that the Princess wear gloves, an accessory not much used in her working wardrobe.

LEFT Traditionally, women wear black when meeting the Pope. The Queen, on her visit to the Vatican, had worn a floor-length black gown with a veil. Diana worked with her designers to dress as appropriately as possible for these occasions. Not only were the black lacy dress and veil appropriate for a Vatican visit, they were also sumptuously detailed.

4

A SENSE OF
OCCASION

Although Diana often felt stifled by the rules and regulations that surrounded royal dress codes, she also enjoyed the sense of occasion and the ceremony of it all. When King Fahd visited from Saudi Arabia, Diana and Charles, as part of their diplomatic duties, met him at Gatwick airport. The Princess had let Catherine Walker go to town on a military-style suit complete with gold braid and frogging. She looked like a drum majorette and was sniped at by one fashion editor for resembling an extra from *Sergeant Pepper's Lonely Hearts Club Band*. Certainly the outfit looked like it had come from the dressing-up box, but then so do many of the Royals' ceremonial robes and suits. She could just as easily forget about pomp and ceremony and wear deck shoes and waterproofs on board *HMS Trafalgar*. Quite 'how a princess should look' was redefined almost every day.

However, when Diana was newly married, 'how a princess should look' was interpreted as 'fairy princess'. Shortly after her marriage, she commissioned Bellville Sassoon to make a romantic ball gown, one of several dresses they made for her that had 'fairy princess' written all

LEFT Diana greeted King Fahd dressed in a white Royal Hussar-style suit, complete with gold frogging, by Catherine Walker. Note the unusual hemline and how the witty frogging theme is carried on to the cuffs and the back of the jacket. Graham Smith at Kangol made the Cossack-style matching hat, finishing it by hand to have it ready in time.

over them. And according to David Sassoon the dress was 'the Queen's idea of how a princess should look'. At the time it was Diana's vision too. Over the years, Diana's vision evolved as she changed and grew up, literally, in the public eye. She made dressing to suit the occasion into an art form, and she very rarely got it wrong, in spite of the diversity of occasion, circumstance, custom and weather.

Each June for Trooping the Colour, Diana put on her wide-brimmed hat and a bow-tied dress or a smart suit, and took her place next to the Queen Mother in a ceremonial coach. Other annual fixtures included Ascot, and of course there were always State banquets or the opening of a ballet to attend and dress for. In 1988, a State banquet at the Elysée Palace in Paris meant a baroque beaded and embroidered duchesse satin gown with bustle and matching bolero by Victor Edelstein; a dress that was so expensive and elaborately decorated that the Princess was later to debate whether or not to include it in the Christie's sale. By the mid-nineties, the serious 'occasion' dresses were pared down, less jewel encrusted and had generally lost their sense of importance and grandeur.

Waterproofs, trousers and deck shoes were exactly right on the wet and rainy deck of *HMS Trafalgar* in August 1986. Diana was always ready to dress the part; for extra warmth she had a sleeveless Puffa jacket underneath.

RIGHT Grey and white was a trusty combination for a service at Westminster Abbey to mark the fiftieth anniversary of the Battle of El Alamein. The Catherine Walker dress and jacket looked smart and classy, without being too sombre or serious. Diana did not often wear gloves, but chose to finish this outfit with gloves and a matching hat by Marina Killery.

LEFT Something old for her brother Charles' wedding in September 1989. Diana wore a grey Catherine Walker outfit that had been seen on at least two separate occasions the previous year – at Ascot and another wedding. The dove-grey jacket, with morning coat-inspired tails, is teamed with a white dress, a wide-brimmed hat, clutch bag and plain court shoes.

Diana didn't mind getting caught in the rain in her Paul Costelloe jacket with diamanté buttons and sequinned lace skirt at Pavarotti's concert in Hyde Park in July 1991. Even the rain could not dampen her glamour and high spirits.

LEFT Diana wore this cream double-breasted dress by Catherine Walker at calf-length as a mark of deference when she visited the Shri Swaminarayan Mandir Hindu Temple, Neasden, in June 1997. She removed her Chanel shoes to enter the temple (*see right*).

ABOVE With a garland round her neck and bare feet revealing dark red nail varnish on her immaculately groomed toes, no detail was ever overlooked. She was happy to adapt to the customs of other cultures with grace and ease.

LEFT For a fund-raising dinner at the Dorchester organized by Imran Khan, Diana wore a beaded and embroidered ivory couture *shalwar kameez* as a tribute to Khan. Glamorous high heels and her signature choker complement the dazzling outfit.

ABOVE Diana's Trooping the Colour outfit in 1989 was a Catherine Walker dress finished with a striped bow at the collar, a double row of buttons to the waist and turned-back cuffs. Topping it all is a hat by Philip Somerville. She wore the same outfit in Melbourne that year.

LEFT Diana wore this softly draped and bowed silk suit by Jan Vanvelden to an earlier Trooping the Colour in 1984. It was one of the few outfits she wore during her pregnancy and afterwards. The wide-brimmed hat was designed by Royal favourite, Frederick Fox.

TROOPING THE COLOUR

ABOVE For the 1987 ceremony, Diana wore a high-collared, tailored cream silk gaberdine suit by Edelstein, which she also wore to Ascot that year. The wide-brimmed Philip Somerville hat is in raw silk with a bow made from the fabric of the suit.

LEFT Diana wore a chic double-breasted suit with black buttons by Catherine Walker to a rainy Ascot in 1991. The black handkerchief, the uncharacteristic black gloves and black hat by Philip Somerville added the final dramatic flourish to a stunning outfit.

RIGHT Diana wore the red and purple Catherine Walker suit and matching hat by Philip Somerville for a sunny Ascot in 1990, an outfit she also wore in Hong Kong and India. Unlike many Ascot-goers, Diana did not always have a new hat made specially for the races.

Diana was still
enjoying her polka
dot phase in 1986
and wore this green
and black suit and hat
to Ascot that year. She
passed the suit on to
her sister Sarah, who
wore it later for a
friend's wedding.

RIGHT This pared-down, belted shift dress by Catherine Walker was worn by Diana on her very last public engagement in the UK.

ABOVE This boat-neck crêpe shift by Catherine Walker was made in several colours because it was such a versatile and flattering dress.

RIGHT A much more up-to-date look for Diana's day wear. This dress by Versace featured zips across the pockets.

ABOVE A velvet jacket, with red satin collar and blue and green lapels, mirrors the rainbow-coloured shift by Tomasz Starzewski, as do jewelled buttons and bright red nails for this rock concert arrival.

LEFT Yellow satin suit by Catherine Walker with black accessories worn to a gala evening in aid of the Prince's Trust at the Palladium in 1990.

ABOVE Diana wore this black-and-white banded nautical-style silk suit with a double row of white buttons by Catherine Walker to a tribute concert for Sammy Davis Jr. at the Royal Albert Hall in 1992.

RIGHT This romantic cream lace dress and satin double-breasted jacket by Victor Edelstein was the perfect outfit for a charity gala ballet performance at Sadlers Wells in June 1990.

BELOW Diana wore
this halter neck,
draped cocktail dress
in grey silk figured
with sequins and
glass beaded
curlicues, to the
Serpentine Gallery in
1995. This Catherine
Walker was bought at
the Christie's sale by
the Fashion Café.

LEFT AND ABOVE
This short Catherine
Walker dress of
midnight blue lace
embroidered with
sequins has sheer
shoulders and back,
and a back button
fastening that adds an
extra dash of
glamour. Diana's
hemlines got shorter
in her later years,
revealing fabulous
long legs.

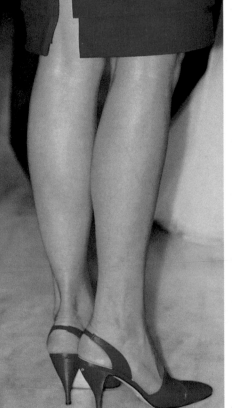

A scarlet formal dress by Tomasz Starzewski with tiered, back-slit skirt detail.

RIGHT A short Catherine Walker dress of fine silk lace with a satin rouleaux halter neck worn on a visit to Argentina, 1995. The heels are high and strappy.

SHORT AND SASSY

RIGHT Diana wore this black chiffon ruched dress with off-the-shoulder straps to a dinner at the Serpentine Gallery on the night of Charles' interview on BBC TV. The short flirty hem and trailing chiffon scarf helped make this Christina Stambolian creation a bit of a show-stopper. Note the famous sapphire and pearl choker, and her sapphire and diamond ring.

LEFT AND ABOVE Diana seized upon this Hachi one-sleeved dress in cream silk chiffon, presented to her by *Vogue* deputy editor Anna Harvey. She wore it to *two* Bond film premieres – *Octopussy* in 1983 and *Licence to Kill* six years later – and in Washington and Australia in 1985. It was bought by *You* magazine at the Christie's auction.

ABOVE Another sensational one-shouldered dress, made of ivory silk crêpe embroidered with pink sequins by Catherine Walker in 1991.

LEFT A fairy-tale chiffon dress with asymmetric hem by Gina Fratini was early Diana, worn to a ballet in Rio de Janeiro. The Princess liked to wear floaty dresses to the ballet.

COUTURE
GLAMOUR

LEFT Diana wore this regal evening gown to a banquet at the Elysée Palace in Paris and at the Winter Garden in New York. It was an elaborate piece of *haute couture* by Victor Edelstein, with duchesse satin bodice and matching bolero. The detailed beadwork using faux pearls and gold beads had been done in Paris. The dress was so elaborate that the Princess limited her jewellery to a simple pair of earrings that had been a wedding present from the Emir of Qatar.

LEFT The back view of the dress reveals the tucked bustle-effect of the skirt as the Princess is greeted by President Mitterrand of France and his wife. The dress was so precious that the Princess could not decide whether to put it in the Christie's sale or not. She did and it sold for almost £55,000, not far off the price it would have originally cost to buy. As with all the dresses sold at the auction, it is now an extremely valuable collector's item.

IVORY TOWERS

BELOW The pearl-encrusted cream 'Elvis' outfit by Catherine Walker was made for a visit to Hong Kong in 1989.

LEFT The Spencer tiara was the stately accessory worn to finish off an ivory spangled dress by the Emanuels. The look is pure Dynasty, with the wide shoulders and the accentuating fan of fabric at one side. The dress was worn to a State occasion in Bahrain in 1986.

LEFT The white silk crêpe dress was a favourite, worn here without the bolero in Budapest and earlier at the British Fashion Awards in 1989.

**RIGHT AND
ABOVE** Diana wore
this eye-catching
Victor Edelstein dress
on at least eight
occasions between
1990 and 1992,
making it an all-time
favourite. The long
thirties-inspired
fuchsia pink silk dress
had a cowl-draped
back and a long
fluid skirt.

RIGHT Catherine Walker made some sensationally sexy dresses for Princess Diana. The neckline of this dress is daringly low and the long skirt kicked out below the knee. She wore this dress, with a diamond necklace, earrings and bracelet given to her by the Sultan of Oman, to a London film premiere in 1995.

RIGHT This evening dress by Catherine Walker of silk taffeta printed with blue chintz flowers was worn in Melbourne in 1988. In spite of all the fussy detail – ruching, side bow and daring side split – Diana carried it off in great style.

BELOW Grecian draped chiffon dress by Catherine Walker, inspired by the movie star glamour of Grace Kelly and worn by Diana to Cannes Film Festival in 1987.

LEFT AND ABOVE Diana's style was becoming more confident and slick by 1989. She wore this sophisticated cream and salmon silk evening dress by Catherine Walker to a first night of *Swan Lake*. Note the plunging back and buttoned cuff details.

5

CASUAL CHIC

UCH OF WHAT MADE PRINCESS DIANA SO POPULAR and well-loved was her modern approach to her own life, both public and private. Not only did she insist on bringing up her children with a sense of reality and a knowledge of the world outside the Palace, she also gave the public a sense that she was not living a rarefied life in her ivory tower by the clothes she wore when off-duty. She strove for a more relaxed attitude within the Royal Family, and the jeans, baseball caps and everyday clothes she wore certainly gave the appearance of a more informal style and a more accessible and human woman. Dressed in that most universal item of clothing, a pair of Levis, Diana was a woman everybody could relate to. She was one of us, dropping in to Jigsaw, Benetton and Marks and Spencers for woollies and T shirts. As with all the great style icons of this century, it was Diana's ability to look cool and chic in the simplest, most everyday clothes that ensures her place, alongside Grace Kelly, Jacqueline Kennedy and Coco Chanel, as a woman who was totally of her time.

A royal wardrobe has two sides to it, one formal and public, the

LEFT AND ABOVE
Wearing informal gingham Capri pants, a man's shirt at Windsor (*above*), or a cerise angora cardigan for off-duty days at Highgrove, must have been a relief after the structured, formal clothing the Princess was expected to wear for her official engagements. She posed for Tim Graham in the summer of 1986.

FAR LEFT Pleated white skirt, big jumper and white woolly scarf were a comfortable choice for travelling with toddler Prince Harry in 1986.

other informal and private. Away from the constraints of protocol, Diana's informal wardrobe was much closer to her own style and the look of the times. She could wear the same casual clothes that other young women around the country wore when they took their children to school or to a movie or theme park. Comfort and ease were the watch words, rather than polish and glamour. Even dresses for her private wear that were commissioned from formal-wear designers like Catherine Walker, David Sassoon and Lorcan Mullany had a completely different feel to clothes by them worn on public occasions.

DENIM DI

Diana looked great in a pair of flat moccasins, fifties-style Capri pants and a baggy white shirt, just as she looked like any other young mum taking her children to school dressed in jeans and a baseball jacket with a pair of cowboy boots. And it was not just Levis; Diana made use of shopping trips to Harvey Nichols where she bought designer jeans too, labels like Versus, the Versace line designed by Donatella Versace, as well as Armani, Gucci and Chanel. In this respect, Diana was very much of the moment, although the fashion press would often criticize her for dressing down too much. She also looked at her most relaxed when she twisted her hair underneath a baseball cap, showing that like most women there were some days when she simply could not be bothered with the fuss of a hair dryer and styling products. The baseball caps, denim jeans and cowboy boots were American influences, which have played a major role in relaxing dress codes in Europe over the last two decades. The great American sportswear ideal, marketed under labels like Ralph Lauren and Banana Republic, was one that the Princess embraced and enjoyed wearing. Once again Diana was breaking down barriers. This was a whole new look for a member of the Royal Family, most of whom formerly liked to keep sportswear firmly on the sports field.

ABOVE Diana strides up the steps of William's school clad in jeans and cowboy boots. A embroidered gold horseshoe on the back pocket adds a whimsical touch. She often wore jeans for the school run or for days out with her children. She had over thirty pairs of jeans, some designer and some plain old Levis. Among her collection were jeans by Margaret Howell, Armani, Versace, Rifat Ozbek and Gucci.

ABOVE Denims again, this time worn with black leather jacket and white moon boots. Prince William is equally casual in jeans, sweatshirt and ski jacket. Diana dressed her children in clothes that any ordinary child would wear.

RIGHT In relaxed mood on the polo field, wearing baseball cap, a man's wool jacket, jeans and cowboy boots in May 1988.

ABOVE AND RIGHT A casual red cardigan over a white dress with a soft knotted bag looked relaxed and informal for a polo match. Diana would drape a jumper over her shoulders when wearing a plain T-shirt or a favourite old skirt, like this print skirt (*right*) from a suit she wore in the days before her marriage. The Provençal patchwork bag was one of five bags (in different designs) that Diana bought from Souleiado's Fulham Road shop.

RIGHT Diana liked
this witty *trompe-l'oeil*
jumper by Roland
Klein, worn with a
long pleated skirt by
Jasper Conran for a
polo match in 1987.
At such times she
dressed William and
Harry informally too.

Diana and Charles walk down the steps of Wetherby School. She often wore a pleated skirt when off duty; Jasper Conran made several for her in fine lightweight wool and wool crêpe in various colours to wear with her casual sweaters. On this occasion Diana teamed the white skirt with a horizontal striped cardigan, a plain white T-shirt and court shoes. Diana's casual wordrobe included several pieces of knitwear by Mondi and Escada.

RIGHT Diana in a wide-belted, longer than usual day dress and two-tone shoes to match, and an equally casual, chino-clad Prince William, after dropping Harry off at Wetherby School, 1990.

ABOVE Diana arrives in Aberdeen on holiday in a Jasper Conran skirt and Mondi jumper with polo player design.

ABOVE Diana wore a belted cobalt blue Jasper Conran jumper for William's first day at nursery school, 1985.

Holidays were an important part of Diana's life. Occasionally she was able to escape the eye of the paparazzi for a few days; something she achieved when the fashion and portrait photographer Patrick Demarchelier lent the Princess his house on the Caribbean island of St Barthelemy. She went with a girlfriend and was allowed forty-eight hours of bliss before she was discovered and the island was invaded by photographers. She then moved to a neighbouring island and the government closed it off so that she could holiday in peace.

Princess Diana was at her most relaxed and carefree while on holiday. The last summer of her life will be remembered as the one she spent relaxing on Dodi Fayed's boat. She took several holidays a year, particularly enjoying sunbathing. As a result, the Princess was able to keep a glowing suntan topped up throughout the year.

Holidays were also a time for family. By 1990 Diana had learned to cope with media attention and the public's unrelenting interest in her and her sons, by agreeing to a photo call at the start of each holiday on the understanding that the rest of the holiday could be spent in peace. For this photo session Diana chose a leopard print swimsuit and matching sarong, exactly what a fashion stylist would have chosen for her to wear, in order to look as exotic as her holiday spot. After that, leopard print swimwear became all the rage. Whatever style she wore was instantly copied and put into production by some enterprising high street store. Of course, Diana's slim, athletic body made her swimwear look fabulous. She bought swimwear from Jantzen and Gottex over the years. The rest of her holiday wardrobe was much the same as anyone else's — lots of plain T-shirts, cut-off jeans and simple plimsolls.

Diana wore bathing suits by Gottex and Jantzen, swimwear specialists. Here on Necker Island, she wore a favourite leopard print swimsuit with a matching skirt to meet the cameras. Jantzen was delighted when Diana began to wear its swimsuits and bikinis on holidays.

LEFT The sculpted look in skiwear – black jacquard Lycra ski pants. The red down-filled jacket is contemporary and unfussy, while the sunglasses give the look of the international jet set.

ABOVE Diana wore her trusty Nordica ski boots and a matching scarf and mitts with a very simple one-piece ski suit. The scarves and headgear were useful for hiding her face from the stares of other skiers.

Winter holidays were often spent skiing, a sport Diana had learned while at finishing school in Switzerland. On the slopes, Diana could forget royal protocol and cultivate her athletic side. Skiwear has had some bad style moments, particularly in the mid-eighties when a pair of salopettes in pink, purple and orange might be worn with an equally garish ski-jacket. For many who ski, the holiday is as much about being noticed for what you wear as for your skiing skills. For Diana, a competent skier, the main criterion was comfort and function. She was not seduced by the flashier designs available, and stuck instead to black leggings, functional waterproof anoraks and sunglasses instead of goggles. Her skiwear was never too flashy or florid, and she wore the same white ski boots year after year. They were comfortable and that's what she wanted. On the slopes she could almost be anonymous. Almost. Diana's ability to turn heads usually gave the game away. She did not look as though she was on the slopes to pose and be seen; she was there to ski. Her fleecy hoods were useful for keeping warm, but were equally good at obscuring her face from people constanting peering at her. Her favourite ski brand was Head, a company that makes functional skiwear, designed for comfort and performance rather than high fashion.

At times, when Sarah Ferguson and Prince Andrew joined the Prince and Princess in the snow, the royal group would make a colourful sight. As with her everyday style, the Duchess of York opted for a more flamboyant style of skiwear, choosing bright colours and joking with the press. Later on, when Prince William and Prince Harry were older, they would often join their mother and other family members on the slopes for winter holidays.

ABOVE Diana often wore reflective sunglasses on the slopes rather than goggles. The photographers found themselves mirrored in the Princess's shades. This one-piece ski suit by Kitex she wore at Klosters in 1987 cost about £300. Diana rang the changes with either pink or white accessories.

LEFT A warm, fleecy hood, goggles and a blue ski suit by Head protect the Princess at Lech, Austria, during a ski holiday in 1992.

RIGHT The Princess bought this and three other Head ski suits from Harrods in fashionable purples and plums. She teamed this with a braided headband at Klosters in 1986. Note the snug, snap-fastened lower sleeves and the asymmetrical front zip closing.

6

LEFT The plane was unloaded at Melbourne airport and Diana's trunks and bags were lined up on the tarmac.

A TRAVELLING
WARDROBE

PLANNING FOR A MAJOR TOUR ABROAD WAS LIKE A MILITARY operation for the Palace, not least when it came to putting together a wardrobe for the Princess that would cover all possibilities of weather change and social function. In 1985 alone the Princess made trips to Italy, Germany, Australia and America. The tour of Australia, in October of that year, was the royal couple's second and involved such diverse engagements as a visit to a building site, a rock concert and a film premiere, as well as the walkabouts that would attract huge crowds, all eager for a smile from the Princess and a glimpse of what she was wearing. After months of work with designers such as Catherine Walker on some new outfits for the trip, and after deciding what in her existing wardrobe would be appropriate, the outfits were packed into wardrobe trunks and chests, each one labelled and numbered.On this tour of Australia and America, Diana took twenty daytime outfits, twelve hats, more than a dozen evening dresses, fifteen pairs of shoes and matching bags, nineteen pairs of earrings, two tiaras, eight necklaces and assorted pairs of tights to match her outfits. Accompanying Diana was her dresser, Evelyn

ABOVE Every piece of luggage was tagged with the Princess's title. Each member of the Royal Family has their own colour-coded luggage label to make sorting easier, particularly when there is a great deal of luggage.

Dagley, who was on hand to help the Princess with her many changes each day. After Australia, the couple flew straight to America. The Princess had meticulously preplanned both trips and unveiled a whole new set of evening gowns, coats and daywear for the visit, including the show-stopping Victor Edelstein dark blue velvet number she wore to the White House dinner and dance hosted by President Reagan.

ABOVE AND RIGHT Throughout the tour, the Princess of Wales' dresser, Evelyn Dagley prepared all the outfits required for the day and evening ahead, including appropriate hats, shoes and bags. Sometimes this would mean changing clothes four times in one day. Diana wore the red Jan Vanvelden coat (she had a similar one in navy blue) and polka dot dress on a day that included a visit to the Botanical Gardens in Melbourne.

BUILDING
SIGHT

Diana wore a blue sunhat but was soon given the regulation hard hat to wear on a Melbourne building site. In typical Diana style, it still matched her outfit. Her suit by Jan Vanvelden in white cotton pique with cobalt blue spots was teamed with a plain white skirt. Diana loved the suit so much she asked the designer to make a copy when drycleaning ruined this one. Note the matching body language between Princess and builder, with their hands in their pockets as they chat informally.

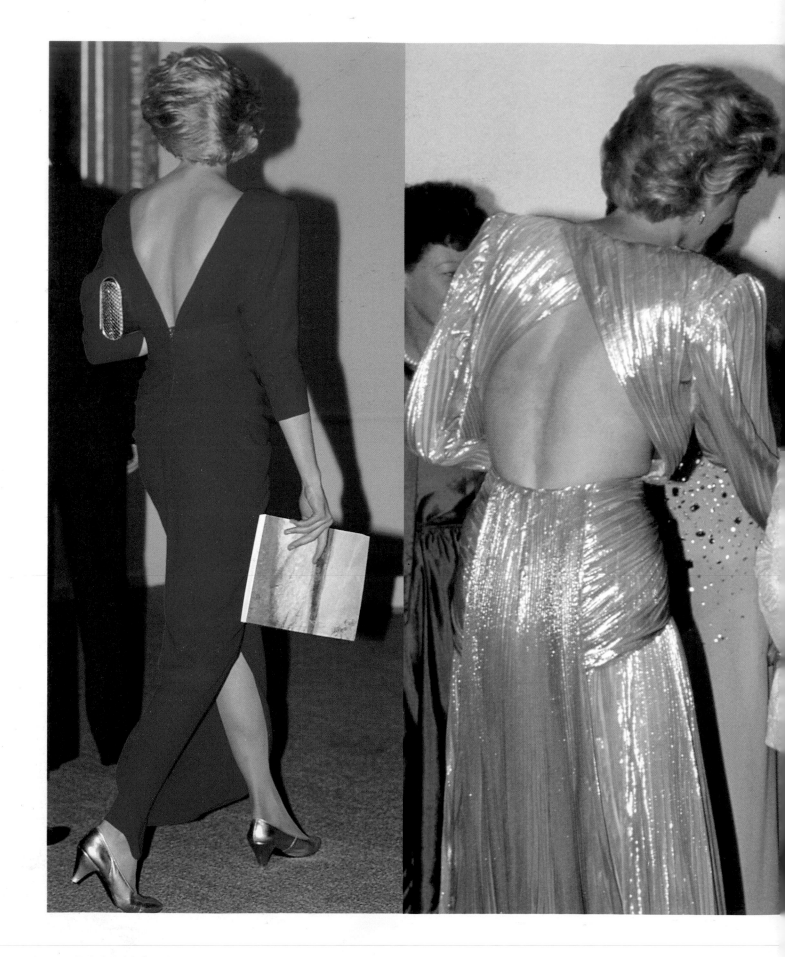

FAR LEFT Diana wore this slim red Victor Edelstein evening dress with silver shoes and bag. The deep V back and side slit are revealing but still elegant.

LEFT Shades of Dynasty for a gala evening in Melbourne in this gold lamé backless dress made for the Princess by Bruce Oldfield. She had to put up with a spot of sunburn on her neck too.

RIGHT Diana caused a stir when she wore a diamond and emerald choker, a wedding gift from the Queen, as a headband with this one-shouldered silk satin organza dress by the Emanuels. She teamed it with emerald earrings, bought by Prince Charles, along with a matching bracelet, from jewellers Wartski as a wedding gift for his bride.

7

EMERGENCE OF STYLE

THE EARLY YEARS

*I*T WAS NEVER A RAGS TO RICHES TALE, BUT DIANA'S TEENAGE years were spent, not in the grand splendour of ribbons and jewels, but in ordinary clothes – jeans and casual jumpers – like most other young girls growing up in the seventies. As a family friend, Prince Charles had seen the young Diana as a child, looking fresh and unsophisticated. During their courtship, Diana's personal appearance was simply an evolution of her teenage self. She wore little make-up, and had not yet perfected the art of dressing for the cameras that were destined to follow her from 1980 to the end of her life. Her dress sense then was far from smart and sophisticated; she favoured the well-worn comfort clothes that suited her position as an assistant at the Young England Kindergarten where she worked full-time. The idea of playing the role of a fairy-tale princess in crinolines and tiaras could not have been further from her mind.

Barely a year later, her engagement to the Prince was announced and Diana's first evening gown was commissioned from the young designers David and Elizabeth Emanuel, who specialized in making one-off party gowns that owed more to historical costume than to fashion trends of the day. The dress plunged front and back and Diana felt smart and sophisticated, particularly because the dress was black, a colour that she thought made her look elegant and grown-up. The

ABOVE A Bellville Sassoon outfit with a bold collar and bow of candy-striped organza.

LEFT At Balmoral before the wedding (*left*); Diana was not yet a Royal and could get away with wearing a folksy Inca jumper over a polo neck, cord trousers by Margaret Howell and a man's watch. Diana's love of colourful jumpers guaranteed their popularity for years.

ABOVE A blue Bellville Sassoon coat with puff sleeves and patch pockets, worn in the early years.

Diana style was on its way, and this was the first of many ball gowns and dinner dresses that she was to have made for her. The second was her wedding dress, the point when the princess began her life as the enduring romantic icon and heroine of the twentieth century.

When Diana's mother Frances Shand-Kydd took her to be fitted out with a trousseau at Bellville Sassoon, David Sassoon remembers Lady Diana Spencer as a young Sloane Ranger, 'a quiet little gauche girl, very shy'; even then, however, she had strong ideas about how she wanted to dress. For her going away outfit, she was adamant that it had to have a straight pencil skirt because she thought that was the smart style to have at the time. From the moment of her engagement, Diana began to dress older than her years, desperately trying to conform to her idea of Royal dressing.

As Diana slowly found her feet in her new role as wife, mother and royal figurehead, so too did she tentatively find her way in a whole new world of occasion dressing, ceremonial costume, tiaras, day dresses and co-ordinated shoes, bags and hats. She enlisted the help of *Vogue* deputy editor Anna Harvey, and began to experiment with a long list of designers, some of whom would make just one or two dresses, and some who were more successful than others. Her look was very traditional and very British during those early years. At times, she was perhaps a little too mumsy-looking, a little too middle-aged and certainly too co-ordinated, wearing a red dress, red tights and a red hat all at once, but her adoring fans were not complaining. It meant she stood out, a radiant beacon in a crowd.

Diana's style in the early years had a certain charm; in 1981 she looked every bit a princess in an off-the-peg Jaeger suit, frilly blouse and John Boyd hat.

LEFT A dramatically tiered taffeta and velvet evening dress in iridescent purple and blue by Catherine Walker was worn with long taffeta gloves during a visit to Munich in 1987.

ABOVE Big hair and big shoulders made Diana pure *Dynasty* in Milan. The draped silk Bruce Oldfield suit was worn with Butler and Wilson earrings with silver bows and crystal hearts.

POWER DRESSING

THE MIDDLE DYNASTY

*A*S THE TWENTIETH CENTURY DRAWS TO A CLOSE, fashion designers are looking back to the eighties as a source of inspiration, revisiting the padded shoulders, the short pencil skirts and high heels, along with the flicked hair and glossy make-up of the period when Diana's style was at its most full-blown. The eye-liner and mascara were bluer than blue, the hair was full and the shoulders of her coats, blouses and dresses were padded and voluminous. Everything about her was slightly larger than life, shinier and glossier, just like the soap operas *Dallas* and *Dynasty*, which were to result in the nickname 'Dynasty Di'. The overriding fashion was gloss and glamour, and that was what British designers like Bruce Oldfield, Catherine Walker and Victor Edelstein were to provide for her in the form of glittery dresses for evening functions, satin blouses with leg-of-mutton sleeves and elaborate bows at the neck.

During this period, Diana became more adventurous with her clothes and would often wear a dress that was positively daring, like the one-sleeved red and black floral print silk taffeta gown she wore to the British Ambassador's banquet in Paris in 1988. The dress, made by Catherine Walker, was an absolute show-stopper, bright in colour and bold in design. By the end of the eighties, the Princess of Wales had developed a keen sense of what would make a great picture and impress her public. She opted for clothes that made her stand out in a crowd. The heavy eye make-up that accentuated her eyes in flash light, and the glossy lips, were just the thing for being photographed.

ABOVE AND RIGHT An unusual hairstyle for Diana was finished with a glittery star and offset the blue satin bodice and skirt by Bruce Oldfield, which she wore several times, including a fashion show at the Sydney Opera House in 1988. Note the witty two-tone shoes with polka dots to match.

RIGHT Diana had not yet come to terms with the less-is-more rule when she wore this orange satin jacket with a black satin bustle skirt and a bow tie to attend the ballet in Lisbon, February 1987.

LEFT Diana liked to cross the boundaries between women's wear and men's wear and wore a bow tie on several occasions. Her hair was swept back behind her ears in forties fashion for a trip to Barnardo's in the East End of London, 1984. She wore two-tone shoes often; the red of her shoes and the red of her poppy make small dramatic splashes of colour against the grey double-breasted Piero de Monzi coat.

LATER CHIC
PARED-DOWN PRINCESS

BELOW AND RIGHT Whether campaigning against landmines in shirt and Armani jeans (*right*) or attending a film premiere in a tight-fitting blue lace dress with plunging neckline by Catherine Walker (*below*), by the mid-nineties, Diana had perfected her new self-confident style. It was clean, chic and minimalist.

*O*VER THE LAST TWO YEARS OF HER LIFE, THE PRINCESS SPREAD HER wings and became international, wearing foreign designers including Versace, Valentino, Ungaro, Cerrutti, Lacroix, Rech, Feraud and Moschino. Her new image was young, confident and slinky. Catherine Walker, ever in tune with the Princess's changing needs and style, designing clothes that were sharper and sleeker than ever before. Now Diana was able to live and dress on her own terms, and her own sense of style was able to shine out. Another British designer she continued to use was Jacques Azagury who made about eighteen glamorous dresses for her. His *piece de resistance* for the Princess was the fitted black beaded dress she wore the night her *Panorama* interview was screened. It had been recorded earlier, leaving her free to attend a function at Bridgewater House in London, wearing Azagury's off-the-peg, low-cut, long black dress, complete with sapphire choker and blood-red painted nails. Azagury watched the transformation from her days of adherence to Royal protocol to her free-spirited independence. 'During those early years, her look was older, partly because that was the look of the times,' suggests Azagury.

Away from Palace protocol, she no longer had to live by the rules and regulations that had earlier been imposed. As she became more

confident, Diana was to break all the rules. She was the first Royal not to wear a hat on formal occasions, not to wear gloves, and at times, to do away with the notion of stockings. She began to choose the sort of clothes she may have been itching to wear for some time. Suddenly she was free to look as she wanted, so she wore necklines that plunged and skirts that showed off her long, shapely legs.

The Diana of the nineties was a woman who was moving with the times, leaving behind the shackles and constraints of the Establishment. She became sleeker and more streamlined, opting for a neat tailored suit for day, the skirt length usually well above the knee and often worn without tights or stockings. Diana now had an all-year tan that meant it was often difficult to tell whether her legs were bare or stockinged. To complement the shorter skirts Diana also took to wearing a higher, finer heel, confident to walk tall at a powerful six feet.

SELF-CONFIDENT AND FREE

Everything about her body language and dress sense pointed to a more assured, self-confident woman, increasingly in control of her own life. She managed to stop biting her nails, often painting them bright red to show them off. Even her hair was to change, her fringe softened and the sides tucked sleekly behind her ears. Indeed, Diana had long-term advice on what to do with her hair from her friend and hairdresser Sam McKnight, who knew precisely every new trend in hair because he was setting the trends. He is one of the fashion world's leading hairdressers, hired by many of the most influential designers to create new and innovative looks for their catwalk shows. Diana followed his advice, and her look by day became that of a fashionable, professional working woman, and by night the look was pure sophistication and unfussy glamour. With a little help from her friend Gianni Versace, Diana became every bit the leader of fashionable society in long lean column dresses that were as sexy as they were fashionable.

LEFT AND RIGHT
In a pale blue short suit by Versace (*left*) or a pale pink suit by Catherine Walker (*right*), Diana's style was at its peak in 1997. She was an international style icon, complete with high-heeled shoes and designer hand-bag. The shorter skirts suited her.

LEFT Perhaps of all the designers, Diana looked her best in Versace. Everything, from the shoes and bag by Jimmy Choo, to her jewellery, matched this stunning purple Versace gown she wore in Chicago.

FAR RIGHT Diana was still wearing one-shoulder dresses in 1996, but now it was a clean and svelte turquoise silk column dress by Versace. Diana wore it to a benefit dinner in Sydney in October.

ABOVE When Diana wore this black velvet halter neck dress designed by Catherine Walker, to a charity function at Versailles in 1994, the low-cut neck-line caused a sensation.

RIGHT For Diana's 36th birthday gala at the Tate Gallery, she wore a long beaded fan-tailed dress given to her as a birthday present by designer Jacques Azagury.

LEFT AND RIGHT
With so many styles to chose from, Diana decided to wear Catherine Walker shift dresses to the preview parties in London and New York to launch her Dresses sale at Christie's. For the London party, she wore an ice blue embroidered cocktail dress (*left*) and for the party in New York she chose a floral, champagne-coloured glass beaded shift; the same dress but in a different colour. The shoes, by Jimmy Choo, had a much higher heel than usual – almost three and three-quarter inches high.

LEFT AND RIGHT
To attend a Pavarotti
concert in Italy during
1995, Diana, ever
the diplomat, chose
to wear white Versace
(*left*); she had a
similar design in
black. For a
performance of *Swan
Lake* by the English
National Ballet, she
wore an ice blue
beaded shift (*right*) by
Jacques Azagury, with
high heels by Jimmy
Choo and opalescent
tights. Diana began
to wear her hair with
a sleek parting, short
fringe and the sides
tucked neatly behind
her ears.

RIGHT The Princess wore a loose-fitting white Versace coat with matching dress to a lunch at Brown's Hotel in London in 1996. She teamed it with sheer black stockings, black shoes and bag.

RIGHT It was not all designer clothing for Diana. She wore this off-the-peg chocolate brown coat with velvet trim by high street name Mansfield on Christmas Day in 1994. It became an instant bestseller.

8

THE DESIGNERS

ELIZABETH AND DAVID EMANUEL

AVID AND ELIZABETH EMANUEL PLAYED A PIVOTAL ROLE IN
establishing the early look of the Princess of Wales.
Her image as a fairy-tale princess, dressed in romantic
frills and lace, was immortalized by the wedding dress
of the century. It had all the elements: the impossibly long train, the
meringue skirts and the frilly neckline. Not surprisingly, thousands of
brides around the world throughout the eighties and into the nineties
wanted a wedding dress just like Diana's.

The pairing of the Princess and the Emanuels was a perfect
combination. Their overblown romantic ideas, never sexy or stodgy,
were just what her youth and innocence demanded. The Emanuels'
light, charming designs may look too feminine and girlie for modern
tastes, but at the time they were the stuff of dreams. The couple had
graduated from the Royal College of Art only four years before they
were commissioned to make a dress for Diana's first royal engagement,
a charity gala. She wore a black taffeta strapless ball gown that showed
too much cleavage; Prince Charles did not approve because it was black,
the official colour of mourning, and it was too low cut. As far as Diana
was concerned however, an Emanuel dress was everything a young
Princess could wish for.

ABOVE Diana's wedding dress by the Emanuels became the most copied dress in history.

LEFT A sequinned tulle dress in pale blue with a pink satin sash was a favourite of the Princess and her public; it was the perfect fairy-princess dress, light, floaty and tull-skirted. Diana first wore it during a visit to New Zealand in 1983. It was sold for over £16,000 at Christie's auction.

BELOW The Emanuels were the first of many designers who were to sit with the Princess on the floor at Kensington Palace with their fabric swatches and sketches spread around them.

LEFT David and Elizabeth Emanuel, the young designers who were to shape the early fairy-tale image of the Princess. Although the wedding dress was their most famous creation, they provided her with a number of outfits, including a blouse that was worn for an official photograph taken by Lord Snowdon for *Vogue* in November 1980.

DIANA'S DESIGNERS

ABOVE Among the outfits Alistair Blair (*above*) made for Diana, was a belted houndstooth jacket trimmed in black, and a matching black calf-length skirt (*above left*) in 1987.

LEFT Couturier Victor Edelstein (*far left*) designed many elegant evening dresses for Diana, including this velvet bustier dress with full-length evening gloves (*left*), worn to a film premiere in 1989. A number of the most glamorous dresses he made for Diana were sold at the Christie's sale to raise money for charity.

ABOVE AND LEFT Jasper Conran (*above*) made some of Diana's daywear in the eighties, including this classic double-breasted green suit (*left*) in 1983.

BELOW Donald Campbell (*below*) designed the lilac silk taffeta evening dress (*below left*) in the eighties. It was later given extra support with a halter neck strap. He also designed the silk crêpe de chine suit worn by Diana to board the Royal Yacht *Britannia* for her honeymoon in the Mediterranean.

ABOVE Victor Edelstein, who made the dress, did not know that Diana was to wear it at the White House until he saw pictures in the press.

THE STORY OF THE EDELSTEIN DRESS

ABOVE Diana and Charles were guests of President and Mrs Reagan. She wore the dress to a banquet and danced with John Travolta that evening.

LEFT AND RIGHT
The ink blue velvet dress, with its off-the-shoulder neckline, had an Edwardian-influenced bow below the waist and a small bustle at the back. Diana wore the dress again, to a State dinner in Germany, with the Spencer tiara.

BELOW Jubilation from the auctioneer Lord Hindlip as the Edelstein dress goes under the hammer for the staggering sum of £133,835, the highest bid at Christie's New York sale of the Princess's collection of dresses. It will be touring in an international exhibition to raise money for charity.

RIGHT The Princess of Wales laughs with designer Bruce Oldfield at a gala for Barnardo's in London 1988. Diana complimented the designer by wearing an Oldfield off-the-shoulder, crushed velvet dress. She brushed glitter make-up on her shoulders for extra sparkle.

RIGHT Diana wore this navy and white silk suit by Roland Klein (*below*) to Ascot in 1987. She also wore it a month later for a walkabout (*right*), with a pair of her ever-faithful two-tone court shoes.

ABOVE AND RIGHT Diana experimented with new designers like Rifat Ozbek (*above*), who made this gold-embroidered moiré taffeta suit (*right*) for a British fashion show at the Ritz in Madrid.

RIGHT Bill Pashley (*below*) designing, cutting and sewing at home in Battersea, made this and many outfits for Diana, her mother and two sisters, including Jane's and Sarah's wedding dresses. Chelsea Cobbler shoes complete Diana's honeymoon outfit.

BRITISH DESIGNERS

*A*s Diana struggled to find her own style, she was to experiment with a long list of British designers, some fresh and dynamic, like the Saint Martin's graduate Rifat Ozbek, and other more established names like Bill Pashley and Roland Klein, who came to London from Paris in the sixties. Some were to dress the Princess only once or twice, while others, including Bruce Oldfield, were to become favourites. That she shopped around indicates just how much Diana enjoyed fashion and searching out new names. She was not content to stick to the old tried and tested favourites of the Royal Family. She wanted to establish a style all of her own.

Bruce Oldfield's designs were glitzy and shiny, perfect for the high-voltage years of the late eighties. His glamorous gowns were part of the Dynasty Di look of the period. Six of his designs were auctioned at the Dresses sale, including the purple crushed velvet off-the-shoulder evening dress that was a favourite of the Princess, worn on several occasions.

LEFT This romantic floaty ball gown by Bellville Sassoon epitomized Diana's early fairy-tale period. The delicate silk chiffon fabric was lightly patterned with hints of pink and blue on white, and tiny flecks of glitter were interwoven for added interest. The off-the-shoulder ruffle, the tiny bows and wide blue satin sash provided the finishing romantic touch.

BELOW
Belinda Bellville and David Sassoon.

BELLVILLE SASSOON

*D*IANA FIRST CAME TO BELLVILLE SASSOON AS A SHY teenager in need of a trousseau. She wore a sailor-inspired outfit by them for the first official photo call with the Queen and Prince Charles after the announcement of the engagement. She soon commissioned a going away outfit from the same designers. After her marriage, Bellville Sassoon submitted sketches to the Princess which she would mark with a 'yes please!' on one dress, or 'this in dark blue please' on another. After Belinda Belville retired, Lorcan Mullany joined David Sassoon.

ABOVE A black lace and white satin cocktail dress, by David Sassoon and Lorcan Mullany, was bought at Christie's sale by *Paris Match* magazine.

RIGHT Lorcan Mullany joined David Sassoon at Bellville Sassoon, which continued designing for Diana.

ABOVE This Bellville Sassoon dress with gold embroidered chain straps and bow at the hips was one of the last dresses they made for the Princess and was sleeker in style than their earlier designs. She wore it to a film premiere in 1991 and to the ballet in 1993.

DIANA'S DESIGNERS

*E*ACH OF THE WOMEN DESIGNERS COMMISSIONED BY PRINCESS Diana over the years had her own specialties. Gina Fratini and Zandra Rhodes are graduates of the Royal College of Art and both designers have strong signatures of their own, with a flare for romantic fairy-tale dresses made out of the lightest of chiffons and silks. Rhodes likes her often beaded and hand-painted creations to be treasured by their owners as works of art, although Diana chose to sell one of her Rhodes dresses and raised over £16,000 for charity.

ABOVE LEFT Gina Fratini, photographed in her studio, is well-known for her love of detail. She designed a number of soft, feminine dresses for Diana, including this ballgown for a banquet in New Zealand, 1983.

ABOVE The cream organza ballgown with lace trim and matching underskirts, has a pin-tucked, scoop-necked bodice and sheer elbow-length sleeves trimmed with lace, fine baby ribbon and bows.

LEFT The Princess chose this suit with puff sleeves and nipped-in waist from Sir Hardy Amies. Caroline Charles (*below*) flanked by a collection of brightly coloured designs.

ABOVE Diana laughs with Zandra Rhodes (*above left*). The pink chiffon and pearl beaded dress with a zig zag hem (*above right*) was worn in Japan in 1986 and was sold at the Christie's sale.

LEFT The Princess with one of the Catherine Walker dresses that was sold at Christie's. The bodice is heavily embroidered with simulated pearls in a paisley pattern. Diana wore this elaborate dress during a trip to Pakistan in 1991 and to a Royal Variety Performance in 1992.

CATHERINE WALKER

RIGHT Diana wore the pink beaded dress with a scarf and large pearl drop earrings while she was in Pakistan. This dress is seen in the main picture in the back row. The skirt is draped sarong-style with an asymmetrical sash from the waist to the hip.

OF THE SEVENTY-NINE DRESSES AUCTIONED BY CHRISTIE'S, ALMOST fifty were designed by the self-taught, French-born Catherine Walker, who worked closely on the Princess's wardrobe for all of her public life. On her last public engagement in the UK, the Princess wore a shift dress by Catherine Walker and she also wore dresses by the designer to the Christie's galas in London and New York. Catherine Walker was the single most important designer in Diana's life and the two enjoyed a very close relationship, supporting each other through illness and crisis. Catherine Walker produced practical dresses for Royal visits and glamorous, up-to-the-minute evening wear. She designed the regal pearl-encrusted column dress and matching bolero with stiff stand-up collar that Diana referred to as her 'Elvis', which sold at the auction for over £90,000.

LEFT The Princess with couturier Catherine Walker and her staff whom she had invited to Kensington Palace. Catherine Walker was recovering from breast cancer at the time and her relationship with Diana was a close one. The designer created so many pieces for Diana over the years that the Princess's style and her wardrobe requirements were to influence Walker's work in general.

RIGHT A dramatic one-sleeved, drop-waisted ballgown shot through with crimson roses was worn by Diana in Paris, 1988. This dress was another Catherine Walker which went under the hammer at Christie's.

ABOVE The Princess talks to Catherine Walker's *petits mains*, some of whom had worked on the Princess's wardrobe for fifteen years.

ABOVE AND RIGHT A fine lace evening coat dress worn by the Princess to France in 1988 and to the Royal Opera House in 1989. Note the contrast between the glamorous dresses and the plain black trouser suits worn by both the Princess and the designer (*above*).

BELOW Couturier Murray Arbeid, now retired, at the cutting table. He made several dramatic and beautiful dresses for the Princess. The finest quality ivory lace (*detail right*) was used for the bodice and sleeves of the gown (*far right*) worn by Diana at a British Embassy banquet in Washington in honour of President and Mrs Bush.

MURRAY ARBEID

LEFT AND BELOW
The shimmery taffeta and lace gown had a scalloped neckline and asymmetrical drop waist. Diana wore Queen Mary's tiara, made by Garrard, and given to her by the Queen, with pearl and diamond earrings, a wedding gift from Collingwood, the jewellers.

LEFT Jacques Azagury in his Knightsbridge salon sketches the red zip dress in silk crêpe de chine that Diana wore to make such a splash in Venice. At their last meeting she made him laugh as she strutted catwalk-style across the floor in the last dress he made for her, which, sadly, she never had occasion to wear.

LEFT Perhaps tempted to go shorter but four inches above the knee was daring enough for her visit to Venice in June 1995. Diana gave Azagury just forty-eight hours to produce this dress that stunned the crowds in Venice.

JACQUES AZAGURY

THE EVENING THAT THE BBC PANORAMA INTERVIEW WAS broadcast, Diana chose to wear a black dress by Jacques Azagury, the British designer who was a great favourite of the Princess. The dress, fabulously fitted and unashamedly flattering, was an important and potent statement. 'It said, "I'm free and I'm going to enjoy myself",' says Azagury. Diana chose Jacques Azagury, whom she met at the London Designers' Exhibition during Fashion Week in 1985, when she was feeling in a playful mood. His dresses were sexy, glamorous and simple, all of which appealed to the new confident Diana. He was largely responsible for shortening the Princess's skirts. 'When I would pin her hems, I would just try to go that little bit shorter. She probably had the most fantastic legs in the world… the best legs.'

RIGHT The low-cut evening dress by Azagury that Diana wore the night her *Panorama* interview was broadcast. A detail of the bodice fabric (*above*) reveals the gorgeous embroidery and the scattering of sequins.

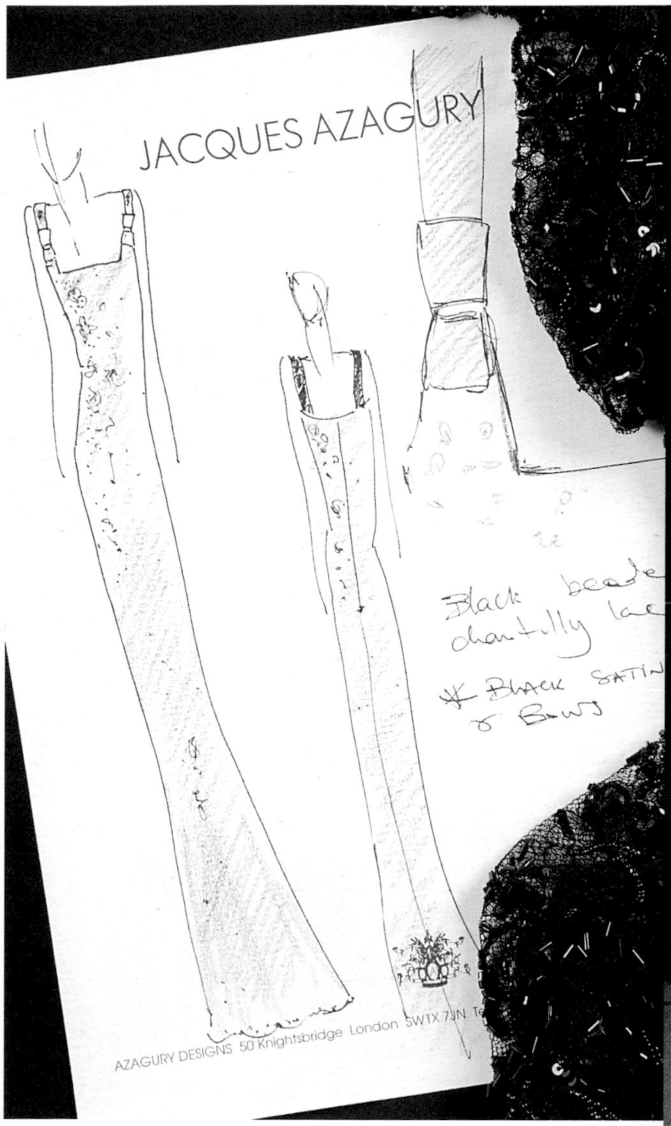
JACQUES AZAGURY
Black beade
chantilly lac
BLACK SATIN
BOWS
AZAGURY DESIGNS 50 Knightsbridge London SW1X 7JN

ABOVE A sketch by Azagury for the black column dress that was to be Diana's birthday present (*above right*), in black chantilly lace. The square neckline and bows are detailed in the sketch.

RIGHT Jacques Azagury gave Diana this dress as a present on her 36th birthday, 1 July, 1997, and she wore it to the gala that evening at the Tate Gallery. It was the same style as the ice blue mini dress she had already worn, but full-length.

LEFT Jimmy Choo at work on a last, making a pattern for a pair of handmade couture shoes. His beautifully crafted shoes were a great favourite with the Princess.

JIMMY CHOO

OVER A PERIOD OF SIX OR SEVEN YEARS, JIMMY CHOO LOST COUNT of how many pairs of shoes he made for the Princess's perfect model-size six-and-a-half. In between the special orders for evening shoes, there were also day shoes in leather and suede to make, and a recurring order for Choo's trademark flat pumps with a 'V' cut out of the front. When the fashion designer Tomasz Starzewski told Choo that he was taking him to meet Diana, he could not sleep that night. Despite the fact that Jimmy Choo's delicate slippers are in demand from royalty and celebrities around the world, a fitting with the Princess was something very special. After that first introduction, the Princess would call Choo direct when she needed shoes to match a particular dress or to take away on a foreign tour. One

RIGHT AND ABOVE The shoe styles Diana wore to the launch parties for the Christie's sale of her dresses. Two pairs were made, in champagne satin and ice blue satin to match the Catherine Walker shifts that she wore. Choo warned the Princess they were high and would be difficult to walk in.

such request resulted in a splendid pair made to match a wonderfully simple but elegant purple Versace gown. He would bring his shoe samples packed in bags and they would sit on the floor and discuss heel shapes and heights, colours and fabrics. As with all her clothes, Diana would always pay for her orders promptly, within two weeks. And when they had decided on the shoes, Diana would help Choo pack the shoes up again and help him carry the assorted bags out to his car. 'I felt very embarrassed,' he recalls. 'I have an old banger of a car.' Typically, Diana made the designer feel at ease when she commented that her sister had exactly the same car.

The story of the Princess and her shoemaker has a poignant ending. Jimmy Choo was to deliver a pair of champagne-coloured V-cut flat shoes – her regulars – on the Monday after the tragedy of the car crash. The last shoes that were hand-made for the Princess were never to reach her and Jimmy Choo would keep them as a remembrance of a very special client and friend.

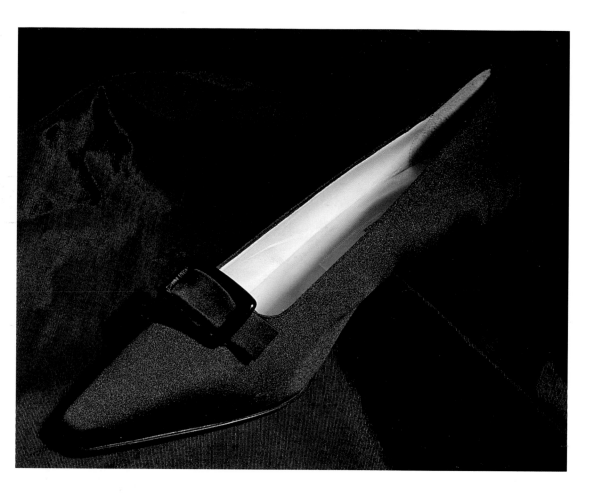

LEFT AND FAR LEFT Jimmy Choo's high-heeled strappy shoes were just the thing to match a red and black military-style dress by Catherine Walker that Diana wore to the Royal Albert Hall in June 1995.

RIGHT Diana called Choo's V-cut flat pumps her 'regulars' and had many pairs in different colours made over the years. They were comfortable and meant she would not tower over her husband and others.

ABOVE Diana had several pairs of Jimmy Choo's classic buckled court shoe. He would visit the Princess at Kensington Palace with bags full of samples for her to try. When they had made a choice, he would make the shoes at his north London workshop.

JOHN GALLIANO AND DIOR

LEFT John Galliano, the latest couturier at the House of Dior, and his sketch of his first dress for Dior to be worn in public by the Princess.

DIANA'S CLOSEST BRUSH WITH HIGH FASHION WAS WITH DIOR when John Galliano was appointed chief designer. Princess Diana made fashion history when she agreed to wear Galliano's first dress for Dior to the annual gala ball at the Costume Institute of New York's Metropolitan Museum in December of 1996. It was over a month before Galliano's first collection for Dior was unveiled, and the fashion world watched with bated breath to see what the madcap genius of British fashion would create for the Princess. The navy blue slip dress was fitted on Diana by Galliano at Kensington Palace and she suggested some modifications. While slip dresses may have been *de rigeur*, the consensus was that they did not suit the Princess's physique, which needed more structure and support.

LEFT The greatest publicity coup in fashion history was made when Diana wore Galliano's slip dress to the Dior gala in New York.

ABOVE The Miss Dior handbag, given to the Princess by Madame Chirac, became another fashion must-have.

RIGHT A Prince of Wales check jacket with frayed lapel edges designed by John Galliano for Dior in 1997. Diana ordered the jacket with both trousers and a skirt. During this last year, she began to wear her hair parted to the side and pushed neatly behind her ears.

LEFT Green military-style suit with belt, brass buttons and epaulettes, by Italian designer Moschino, diplomatically chosen for a visit to Britain by the Italian President and later worn during a visit to Japan.

RIGHT AND BELOW Pale blue bouclé suit by Louis Feraud has the shorter skirt length, and the fashion house's signature buttons. Diana wore this in Japan as well.

LOUIS FERAUD AND MOSCHINO

CHANEL

LEFT AND ABOVE

Pale green Chanel suit, with the distinctive crossed 'C' buttons, worn on St Valentine's Day, 1997. Diana carried a favourite black Chanel bag (*above*) on many occasions, including the trip to Japan where it made an appearance with the pale blue Louis Feraud suit (*far left*).

LEFT The Princess
wore John Boyd's
floppy brimmed pale
pink hat with fabric
feather trim on a visit
to Sicily in 1985.

MILLINERS

JOHN BOYD

THE PRINCESS'S EARLY LOVE OF FEATHERS AND FRILLS WAS fuelled partly by the millinery creations of John Boyd, the Scottish-born hat designer. His small skullcap hats sat close to her head, usually with a neat plume of feathers or corsage of flowers, or a veil covering her face. The Princess loved a veil and enjoyed wearing hats, especially if they were small enough to sit on her head without obscuring her fringe. Introduced to him by her mother, Diana looked to him for most of her early hats. She didn't always know how to wear them, but he encouraged the 'wee bit of a lass' as he called her, and built her confidence. She did a huge amount to boost the hat industry and 'Lady Di' hats were much in demand.

ABOVE On the tour
of Australia in 1985,
Princess Diana
learned to secure her
hats with a comb
hidden inside the
brim. She loved to
wear a veil and it
became part of the
early Diana style. This
hat was teamed with
a lavender wool
crêpe dress with
scalloped sailor collar
by Jan Vanvelden.

RIGHT Hats must look good from all angles. This John Boyd design with a silk rosette to one side was also made in turquoise. It is teamed with a silk crêpe de chine three-piece suit in banana, fuchsia and royal blue stripes by David Neil and Julia Fortescue, worn on Diana's Australian tour of 1983.

ABOVE The Scottish milliner John Boyd in his Knightsbridge shop, surrounded by some of his creations. His hats are worn by several members of the Royal Family, including the Queen.

LEFT Flying saucer hat in maroon with white trim, worn in Italy in 1985, matched a striped and bowed dress by Victor Edelstein. The pearl choker was very much in evidence during the middle years of the decade.

MILLINERS

FREDERICK FOX

HOLDER OF A ROYAL WARRANT AS MILLINER TO the Queen since 1974, Frederick Fox was a logical stop for the young Princess of Wales. A milliner from the tender age of twelve, he came to London from Sydney via Paris and began creating hats for the Queen in 1969, and was granted a Royal Warrant five years later. He has made hats for several other members of the Royal Family, including Diana. She began to wear Frederick Fox's wide-brimmed hats in the mid-eighties, making a move away from John Boyd's neat little feathered and veiled numbers. He works with couturiers such as Hardy Amies and Jasper Conran, and designers Red or Dead, as well as producing designs for films and television productions.

ABOVE Diana wore this peach and white hat with a simple bow around the crown at Ascot in 1985, to match a peach silk Jan Vanvelden suit. She wore the suit while pregnant then had it revamped along slimmer lines.

RIGHT Frederick Fox in his Bond Street studio with the Queen's block in the foreground. Each client has her own block so that Fox can mould the hat to fit perfectly each time. From his showroom he creates his exclusive designer range of hats, but he also has a boutique collection of inexpensive hats in velvet and straw.

ABOVE Surrounded by a selection of the wide brimmed hats that he enjoys designing, Frederick Fox also worked on hats for movies including *2001, A Space Odyssey*.

MILLINERS

PHILIP SOMERVILLE

ABOVE LEFT This wide-brimmed hat originally featured a bow to match a dress that fastened with a bow. Diana wore a series of straw hats in Australia against the sun and the heat.

ABOVE A millinery no-no according to the designer himself. This turban hat, made to go with an Escada coat in 1987, was not one of Philip Somerville's great favourites.

*A*T THE FUNERAL OF THE PRINCESS OF WALES, HER mother Frances Shand-Kydd wore a black, wide-brimmed hat originally designed by Philip Somerville for the Princess herself to wear to the memorial service for her father. The hat was typical of the elegant, classic shape Somerville was to design for Diana when she first came to him in 1986 after seeing one of his hats on television. It was what he calls her 'grown-up period' when she wanted to move on from the fussy style of hats that were traditional to the Royal Family. Philip Somerville took over where John Boyd left off. 'I changed the look,' explains Somerville, leafing through the book of sketches he built up for Diana over a period of ten years. 'I was the guy that put the Princess into big hats.'

Philip Somerville's hats are classic and at times his creations were

bold and daring too. The blue quilled turban (*page five*) with a white brim was a brave move, involving the famous fringe being swept away from her face. But a particular favourite for her was the Jackie Kennedy pill box worn pushed to the back of her head. For every outfit, Somerville would present Diana with six or seven mock-ups and they would fit each one and decide on the final design between them. He would visit Kensington Palace for fittings about four times a year, although in the early days, she would visit the salon in central London herself and occasionally pick something from off the peg. 'Of course, it won't fit me,' she would joke. 'My head's too big.'

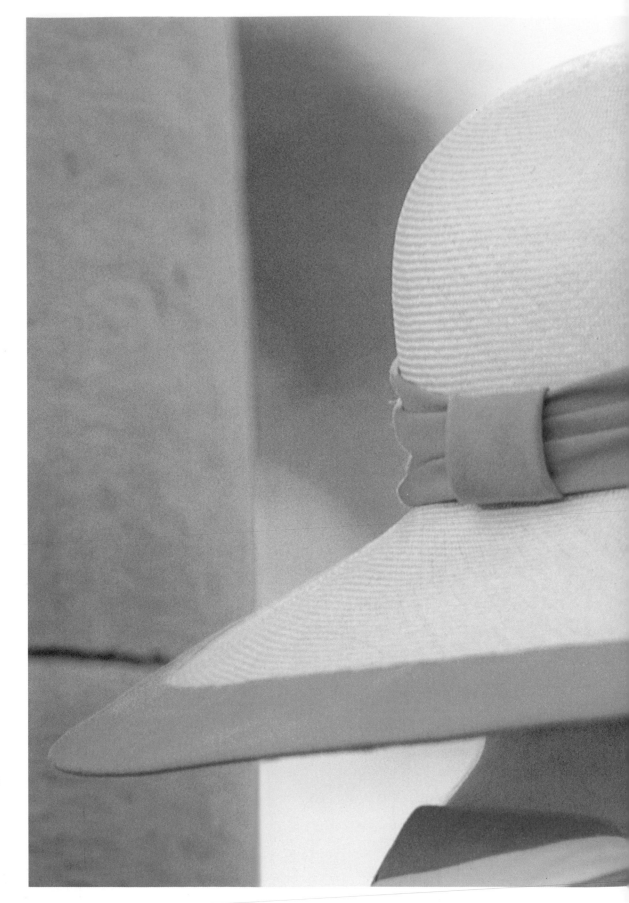

This wide-brimmed, flamboyant blue and white hat is typical of Philip Somerville's work for the Princess. It was worn on a trip to India in February 1992; with such a wide brim it was guaranteed to keep the sun off her face. Somerville once remarked that she could wear a particular hat he designed for her last Australian tour while off-duty but the Princess was almost horrified by the suggestion, since she never wore a hat when not working if she could get away with it!

GRAHAM SMITH

ABOVE The milliner Graham Smith produces his own model collection but also designs hats for Kangol. Greatly in demand for weddings and Ascot, he made a number of hats for Diana over the years.

LEFT A neat beige hat with black pom-pom by Graham Smith reflected Diana's sense of fun and humour. It was worn here to match a suit by Arabella Pollen on a regimental visit.

MARINA KILLERY

RIGHT
A wide-brimmed lampshade-style hat framed Diana's face perfectly at the wedding of Viscount Linley and Serena Stanhope. A rose-filled brim (*below right*), described teasingly by the press as her 'Spanish donkey' hat added a pretty, romantic touch for Ascot. Marina Killery began to make hats for Diana after Anna Harvey, deputy editor at *Vogue*, showed them to the Princess. Diana chose three hats on that occasion and came back for more. Marina Killery's work is theatrical and romantic, and very much in demand for weddings and Ascot.

MAKING CHANGES

THREE HATS, TWO JACKETS AND ONE SKIRT...

BELOW A black, side-buttoned Bruce Oldfield skirt with peplum jacket and headband, worn in Vancouver, 1985.

DIANA DID NOT BELIEVE IN WEARING A DRESS ONCE AND then casting it to the back of her wardrobe. Like most members of the Royal Family, she was mistress of the fine art of recycling clothes to fit different occasions or different moods. Not only would Diana get the most out of her wardrobe by reconstructing outfits to match a jacket with different skirts, changing a hat, or wearing the same skirt with various styles of jacket, she would take clothes back to the designer to be taken in, shortened, or remade altogether into a new dress for a new occasion. The same jacket, skirt or dress would crop up again and again, year after year, sometimes simply worn in a different way; at other times transformed almost beyond recognition. Diana herself would experiment with the way she wore her clothes and would suggest alterations. She also had old faithfuls, clothes that she felt comfortable in and that could always be relied upon.

David Sassoon transformed a floral maternity dress into a smart day dress by clever recutting and fitting, and even her pink going-away suit was given a longer life than just the evening of her wedding. Diana, ever practical, had asked Sassoon to make two jackets for the suit, one short-sleeved and the other long-sleeved, in case it was a cold day. On

ABOVE Stockings with seams and ankle bows caused some comment when she arrived at the races.

her Australia tour, she wore the long-sleeved jacket that had not yet been seen. One of Sassoon's print 'working' dresses was such a hit that it didn't even have to be altered for the Princess to wear it over a period of five years.

It was an endearing trait that the Princess, who hardly needed to scrimp and save, saw fit to extend the life of her clothes. 'She was never extravagant,' says David Sassoon. 'She was always sensible, and she got that from her mother.' While changing the hem line of a dress is nothing new, Diana was inventive in the way she put her clothes together and reworked outfits. A particular suit could be made to look completely different with the addition of some new trim, or even just a bright new hat. A peplum would appear or disappear on a dress giving a whole new look, or a ball gown would be sent back to the designer for a major overhaul, and return barely recognizable as the same dress. One such ball gown was an elaborate beaded and embroidered Catherine Walker dress, worn for a trip to Qatar in 1986. In keeping with local customs, the dress was cut high at the neck and had long sleeves. Three years later however, Ms Walker's team recut the dress with a sexy sweetheart neckline, removed the sleeves and much of the top half of the dress. The same dress now looked chic and glamorous.

HAT TRICKS

Hats too, got the rigorous Diana treatment. Philip Somerville's workshop was kept busy with adjustments to existing hats as well as creating new ones. The pink and violet hat with a pagoda-shaped crown that matched a Catherine Walker suit for Diana's Hong Kong trip, was given a flat crown on her return. And the Catherine Walker suit reappeared several times after the Hong Kong trip. Most memorably, Diana wore it with a smartly shortened skirt to pose for photographers outside the Taj Mahal, this time without the hat.

ABOVE
Diana customized the Moschino houndstooth jacket with contrasting trim laced through the lapels and cuffs to give it a fresh look in February 1992. Without the hat and with a scoop neck top it took on a more casual look.

LEFT The Princess of Wales wore the Moschino suit with its original matching trim at Sandringham during Christmas, 1990. She teamed it with a hat, gloves and a polo neck for warmth. Diana wore the suit again, with its original trim intact during a tour to Canada in 1991.

LEFT The Princess used all the elements of her wardrobe to their full extent. If she had several hats, coats and suits in a similar shade, she would mix and match the elements to suit different occasions. In Sheffield (*left*) she wore a fussy striped bow blouse under a blue wool coat, both by Bellville Sassoon, with a net-trimmed hat by John Boyd.

MIX AND MATCH

ABOVE LEFT Later, in Washington, she wore a more fitted blue Bruce Oldfield dress that had a black cummerbund detail at the waist, with a blue and black hat to match. On another occasion, she wore the Bellville Sassoon coat (*above*) with a neater neckline and a dickie bow topped with the black and blue hat she had worn in Washington.

RIGHT Earlier, in 1983, she had worn the John Boyd net-trimmed hat with a blue wrapover wool coat dress with contrasting black trim on collar and cuffs by Catherine Walker. The coat featured puff sleeves and a high mandarin collar. Pieces of the wardrobe would reappear in different combinations time and time again

RIGHT The Princess of Wales wore an elaborately beaded and embroidered dress made by Catherine Walker for a visit to Qatar in 1986. The eggshell blue evening dress with long sash that tied at the back, had a high neck and long sleeves in keeping with local customs.

RIGHT By March 1989, Diana had given the same dress a major overhaul. Gone were the heavy neckline and long sleeves. The remade dress looked sleek and glamorous and the Princess wore it on several occasions after that.

RIGHT Diana wore this cummerbund-wrapped, wide-skirted evening dress to Claridges in March, 1989. It looked formal but fussy. The bodice fastened at the back and was embroidered with mauve violets and pink roses of silk and chenille.

RIGHT The dress was remade and vastly improved by designer Catherine Walker for a visit to Korea in 1992. The bodice had been transformed into a bolero, worn over a lilac column dress. It was too fine a piece to be cast aside and was sold at Christie's for £31,000.

LEFT AND RIGHT
Designer Victor
Edelstein once said of
Diana 'The Princess is
quite thrifty with
clothes. They often
come back and we
remodel them,
shorten them or
restyle them. But if we
cut them in shreds
they would still look
spectacular on her.'
A polka dot day dress
by Edelstein is seen
with a formal hat and
a peplum at the 1986
Derby (*left*). Both hat
and peplum had
disappeared in June
1987 (*right*) when
Diana presented a
polo trophy to Major
Ronald Ferguson,
father of the Duchess
of York. The peplum
was apt to fly around
in the wind.

10

THE DETAILS

*T*HE TINY DETAILS AND TRADEMARKS OF DIANA'S LOOK ARE AS instantly recognizable as the whole outfit itself. Over the years, Diana built up a repertoire of trademarks, from the blue eyeliner of the eighties to the obvious Spencer tiara, and the string of pearls worn tight to the neck. Diana's accessories were a key part of any outfit and she relished the finer details of her clothes, shoes and jewellery — the way a dress buttoned up the back, the beading on a garment or a feather on a hat. The small things made a difference.

Just as Diana was groomed from head to toe, she would never be seen in public without the right earrings and matching necklace, or the right shoes and bag. Often, however, the jewellery was purely costume. The Princess loved to wear fake baubles and leave people guessing if they were real or not. Perhaps her most important accessories were the sapphire and diamond engagement ring and matching earrings or the sapphire, diamond and pearl choker that became her signature pieces.

FROM LEFT TO RIGHT Bow detail on the front of a royal blue evening dress by Catherine Walker; jet buttons on the back of a red silk crêpe dress by Victor Edelstein; a contrast of textures: a lacy panel on a navy velvet dress; blue satin collar, cuffs and belt on a dress worn in Egypt in 1992.

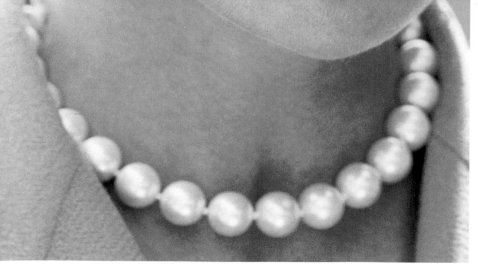

ABOVE The famous nineteenth-century Spencer tiara of diamonds on gold and silver (*above*) is a family heirloom; a single strand of pearls, a Diana trademark (*left*). She loved to mix costume jewellery with her precious gems.

ACCESSORIES AND ECCENTRICITIES

ABOVE Small dark sunglasses worn with a Bellville Sassoon dress in Seville, 1992. Diana wore this print summer dress on many occasions and it remained a personal favourite for several years. David Sassoon called this her 'caring' dress.

ABOVE Diana wore white larger framed sunglasses with a long-skirted pale pink Edina Ronay suit. Large pearl earrings, a few simple bangles and a single strand necklace complete Diana's simple, elegant look.

ABOVE The eighties saw the arrival of puffball skirts. This striped version was designed by Catherine Walker and was worn at Cannes, 1987 with classic two-tone shoes. Diana had two puffball skirts.

ABOVE Polka dots were a favourite with Diana in the eighties. She caused a stir when she turned up at a polo match in a Mondi polka dot skirt and matching ankle socks worn with red high heels.

ABOVE AND ABOVE LEFT Pearls, pearls, pearls – single, double, treble strands, worn tight to the neck or hanging long and loose. Diana wore her pearls back to front once and later reported regretting this fashion statement because the knot dug into her back as she sat through a film premiere.

LEFT Diamond and pearl encrusted brooch worn on a sash. Diana often wore her jewellery in unconventional ways. After the auction, the jewels from the cream Victor Edelstein dress were removed and sold individually to raise even more money for charity.

SIGNATURE JEWELLERY

BELOW Amethyst earrings and pearl choker matched the colour of the purple Versace dress Diana wore in Chicago, June 1996.

ABOVE
The large sapphire was an engagement present from the Queen Mother, and is supposed to have cost £28,500. Diana had it set in a brooch surrounded by diamonds, and later had the brooch mounted on a pearl choker. The sapphire earrings can be worn with or without the drop circlet.

OVERLEAF
Close-up back view of the pink rose and bow that trimmed this pretty pink wide-brimmed hat by Philip Somerville that Diana wore to Ascot, 1989.

11

THE LEGACY

On a sombre September morning, at a press committee meeting for the British Fashion Council held at Vogue House less than two weeks after the death of Diana, Princess of Wales, and chaired by her friend and sartorial advisor Anna Harvey, the question was mooted of how the Princess's memory could best be commemorated by the British fashion industry. The Princess had supported British fashion even after her divorce when she was free to shop wherever she pleased; the loss of one of the industry's most fabulous ambassadors will be deeply felt. Her relationships with the designers she had patronized over the years often went deeper than is usual between designer and client. Many considered her a friend. Those I talked to while researching this book all spoke of her kindness, her radiance and her sense of fun and good humour. She seemed genuinely to enjoy wearing the clothes they made for her and appreciated their skills and craftsmanship. To each of them she was totally unique, and they all commented on how she would, without fail, send thank you notes and little gifts after she had worn an outfit which she always insisted on paying for, and promptly too.

'The Princess had such a sense of humour. She was absolutely divine, very charismatic and very special,' said David Sassoon. 'She was the perfect woman to dress in every sense,' agreed Jacques Azagury. 'No one has ever been quite as popular as Princess Diana. Around the world she was completely universal; there is nobody to take her place.' Diana never wore the last dress that Azagury made for her, a long black gown to be worn to a film premiere in October.

Diana herself had only recently mourned the death of her friend, Gianni Versace. Now it is the fashion world's turn to mourn the death of a Princess. Over the years, Diana had worn the clothes of British-based designers Azagury, Victor Edelstein, Bruce Oldfield, David and Elizabeth Emanuel, Zandra Rhodes, Roland Klein, Rifat Ozbek, Edina Ronay, Murray Arbeid, Bill Pashley, Amanda Wakeley, Caroline Charles, Gina Fratini, Bellinda Bellville, David Sassoon and Lorcan Mullany, Tomasz Starzewski, Anouska Hempel, Kanga and of course, the designer who formed the backbone and heart of Diana's wardrobe and style, Catherine Walker. These are not the designers who have made London the most important international fashion centre since the sixties, but the designers who quietly carry on providing a personal service to their loyal customers while younger, cutting-edge British fashion design is hyped around them. It is quite fitting then that the British Fashion Council agreed to help and support future generations of fashion designers with an annual bursary in her memory, by sponsoring one graduate annually

through a post-graduate Fashion MA. Also fitting is the Gala Tribute in Dress to Diana, featuring the dresses of many of the designers who worked with the Princess over the years, to raise money for the Memorial Fund. The dresses she sold to raise money for charity continue to raise money: American boutique owner, Maureen Rorech bought fourteen of the dresses, including the Victor Edelstein dress. Since Diana's untimely death, she has set up the People's Princess Charitable Foundation, which has organized an international tour of the dresses in order to raise money for charities including the Red Cross, the American Cancer Society, landmine victims and various AIDS organizations.

At the British Fashion Awards in October 1997, Bruce Oldfield paid tribute to the Princess as 'a dear friend and a staunch ally'. 'As well as having fun, she genuinely wanted to play her part in our success,' he said. 'Her awakening to the pleasure of clothes and clear enjoyment in wearing them helped raise awareness of fashion.' What is sure is that there is no woman of style to take the place of Diana as a supreme icon. There is no one with her dynamism, her charisma and her ability to charm and inspire love from all levels of society as she did. Newspapers and society magazines are still publishing archive pictures of the Princess on their covers and still, people want to read about her. Those mourning her outside the gates of Kensington Palace in the days before her funeral all spoke of Diana's beauty, as though it was unthinkable that somebody so beautiful should be removed from their lives.

Diana hoped that one day she might be remembered as a modern-day Jackie Kennedy. The two women's lifestyles were more linked than she realized, from the constant commentary and fascination with the clothes they wore, to the love of couture and jewellery, and the similarities of classic style, both in public and informal situations. Neither of them was much interested in fashion novelties, preferring, in Diana's later years at least, clean classic lines, the secret of style that doesn't date and an image that will endure the test of time. When Philip Somerville designed a pillbox hat for Diana, she was thrilled that she could wear it in the style of Jackie Kennedy, pushed to the back of her head with her fringe showing as she liked. 'I think she'll be *more* important than Jackie Kennedy,' says Somerville with conviction. 'She was such a kind person; she wasn't just a clothes-horse. She glowed warmth. We miss her terribly.'

Diana looked natural and unselfconscious in a sleeveless chambray shirt with Armani jeans and J P Tod moccasins as she campaigned against landmines in Angola, January 1997. She had fulfilled her aim in life to become a 'work-horse' not a 'clothes-horse'.

INDEX

AMC Romance 7
Amies, Sir Hardy 153, 174
Arbeid, Murray 7, 14, 158–9, 203
Armani 104, 132, 205
Azagury, Jacques 15–16, 58, 132, 136, 139, 160–63
  on Diana 15–16, 132, 161, 202

Bashir, Martin *see Panorama* interview
Bates, David 173
Bellville, Belinda 9, 150, 203
  see also Bellville Sassoon
Bellville Sassoon 9, 42, 68, 124–6, 150–51, 182–3, 186–7, 196
  see also Bellville, Belinda; Sassoon, David
Blair, Alistair 144
Blahnik, Manolo 23
Boyd, John 39, 126, 172–3, 174, 176, 186–7
  on Diana 172
British Fashion Council 202, 203
Butler and Wilson 128

Campbell, Donald 145
Cerrutti 132
Chanel 19, 23, 58, 104, 171
  bags and shoes 23, 53, 76, 171
Chanel, Coco 102
Charles, Prince of Wales 142
  Dimbleby interview 6, 13, 34
  jewellery gifts to Diana 13, 49, 91, 123, 194

Charles, Caroline 5, 14, 43, 153, 203
Chelsea Cobbler 149
Chelsea Design Company 8
Choo, Jimmy 9, 11, 23, 136, 138, 139, 164–7
  on Diana 166
Christie's (New York), Dresses sale 6–8, 14–17, 69, 89, 91, 93, 138, 143, 147, 149, 152–5, 191, 198
  parties 16–17, 23, 138, 154, 164
Coffin, Donna 7
Collingwood 159
Conran, Jasper 14, 107, 109–10, 145, 174
Costelloe, Paul 54, 74

Dagley, Evelyn 118–19
Demarchelier, Patrick 6, 14, 112
Dior, Christian/House of 11–12, 45, 54, 168–9
Dresses sale *see* Christie's (New York)
Duke, Roxanne 7

Edelstein, Victor 7, 14–15, 28, 35, 69, 79, 87, 95, 98, 123, 129, 144, 174, 192–3, 194, 198, 203
  on Diana 14–15
  White House dress 6–7, 15, 119, 146–7, 204
Elizabeth, Queen 173, 174–5, 177
  gifts to Diana 123, 159
Elizabeth, the Queen Mother 199

Emanuel, David and Elizabeth 32, 34, 97, 123, 124, 142–3, 203
  Diana's wedding dress 14, 126, 142–3
Escada 28, 58, 109, 176

Fashion Café 7, 89
Feraud, Louis 132, 170–71
Ferragamo 50
Forge, Gilly 31
Fortescue, Julia 173
Fox, Frederick 28, 65, 78, 174–5
Fratini, Gina 6, 93, 152, 203
Freedman, Michael 7

Gabbay, Alexander 23
Galliano, John 11–12, 168–9
Garrard 159
Gina 23, 53
Gottex 112
Graham, Tim 9, 61, 103
Greenwell, Mary 14
Gucci 104

Hachi 93
Hempel, Anouska, 203
Harry, Prince *see* William and Harry, Princes
Hartnell, House of 6
Harvey, Anna 13–14, 93, 126, 181, 202
  on Diana 14
Harvey Nichols 104
Head 115, 117
Henry, Prince *see* William and Harry, Princes
Hindlip, Lord 147
Horyn, Cathy 8

Howell, Margaret 104, 125

Ivory 23

Jaeger 126
Jantzen 112
John, Elton 11
Jourdan, Charles 23

Kanga 203
Kangol 37, 69, 180
Kelly, Grace 63, 100, 102
Kenar, Ritu 60
Kennedy, Jacqueline 54,
    102, 177, 204
Khan, Imran 77
Khan, Jemima 60
Killery, Marina 31, 51, 72,
    181
Kitex 115
Klein, Roland 14, 107,
    148–9, 203
Knowlands, Viv 183

Lacroix 132
Lauren, Ralph 104, 105
Levis 104

McEnroe, Kate 7
Mackenzie, Graeme and
    Briege 6
McKnight, Sam 14, 134
Mansfield 140
Margaret, Princess 16
Martin, Richard 8
Miss Dior 169
Mondi 109–10, 197
Monzi, Piero de 31, 131
Morgan, Christopher 183
Moschino 132, 170, 184–5
Mullany, Lorcan 9, 104,
    150–51, 203

Oldfield, Bruce 14, 123,
    128–30, 148–9, 182–3, 187,
    203

on Diana 204
Onassis see Kennedy,
    Jacqueline
Ong, Benny 14
Ozbek, Rifat 14, 104, 148–9,
    203

Panorama interview 13, 34,
    132, 161–2
Pashley, Bill 149, 203
People's Princess Charitable
    Foundation 204
Pollen, Arabella 31, 180

Rayne 23
Rech, Georges 132
Red or Dead 174
Rhodes, Zandra 152–3, 203
Rock and Royalty 11
Ronay, Edina 14, 196, 203
Rorech, Maureen 204

Sassoon, David 9–10, 42, 69,
    104, 150–51, 182–4, 203
    on Diana 9–10, 42, 126, 184,
    196, 202
    see also Bellville Sassoon
Shand-Kydd, Frances 9, 126,
    172, 176, 184
Shilton, Clive 23
Smith, Graham 37, 69, 180
Snowdon, Lord 14, 143
Somerville, Philip 9, 27–9,
    44, 49, 58, 63, 78–9, 80–81,
    176–9, 184, 199
    on Diana 34, 63, 204
Souleiado 106
Spencer tiara 97, 147, 194–5
Stambolian, Christina 6, 13,
    91
Starzewski, Tomasz 14, 49,
    86, 90, 164, 203

Tatters 65
Testino, Mario 8
Tilberis, Liz 11, 13

Tod, J. P. 23, 205
Travolta, John 6–7, 146

Ungaro 132

Valentino 132
Vanvelden, Jan 37–8, 47, 78,
    119–21, 172, 174
    on Diana 47
Versace, Donatella 104
Versace, Gianni 10–11, 14,
    20, 23, 45, 52, 54, 84, 104,
    132, 134–6, 139, 140
    purple dress (1996,
    Chicago) 11, 166, 199
Versus 104
Vogue 13–14, 143
    see also Harvey, Anna

Wakeley, Amanda 14, 203
Walker, Catherine 7, 8–9,
    14, 16–17, 20, 24–9, 34–7,
    39–41, 43–5, 48, 50, 53,
    55–6, 60–63, 67, 68–9, 72–3,
    76, 78, 80–81, 84–90, 93, 97,
    99, 100, 118, 128–9, 132,
    135–8, 154–7, 164, 167, 184,
    187–91, 194, 197, 203
    'Elvis' outfit 97, 154
    friendship with Diana 9,
    43–5, 154–7
    photographs with staff 9,
    154–6
    Qatar dress 184, 188–9
    Taj Mahal outfit 12, 177,
    184
Wartski 122
William and Harry
    (Henry), Princes 8, 102–5,
    107, 110, 115

York, Sarah, Duchess of 115
You magazine 93
Yuki 58, 63

First published in GREAT BRITAIN in 1998
by WEIDENFELD & NICOLSON

Text copyright © TAMSIN BLANCHARD, 1998

The moral right of TAMSIN BLANCHARD to be identified
as the author of the text of this work has been asserted
in accordance with the COPYRIGHT, DESIGNS
AND PATENTS ACT of 1988

Photographs copyright © TIM GRAHAM, 1998

Design and layout copyright
© WEIDENFELD & NICOLSON, 1998

A CIP catalogue record for this book is
available from the British Library

ISBN 0 297 82432 5

Art Direction by: DAVID ROWLEY
Designed by: NIGEL SOPER
Typeset in: FUTURA, SHELLEY & SPECTRUM
Edited by: MARILYN INGLIS

WEIDENFELD & NICOLSON
THE ORION PUBLISHING GROUP LTD
5 UPPER SAINT MARTIN'S LANE
LONDON WC2H 9EA

ACKNOWLEDGEMENTS

Our thanks to all those designers who gave
their help. As the Princess had such an
extensive and varied wardrobe, it would be
hard to find a designer whose outfits had not
been worn by the Princess at some time;
however, it would be impossible to include
every one of them in any one book. Our
apologies, therefore, to anyone who thinks
they should have been included. We will
have to feature you in a follow-up volume!

Thanks too, to Eileen Graham and her team
– Melissa Tarafa, Vivien Hoobs and Kate
Bennett – for their invaluable help with so
much of the research.

Nigel Soper's design for the book has given it
a stylish, unique quality and he coped
admirably with the volume of pictures and
mass of detail.

And finally, a huge thank you to Marilyn
Inglis for editing the book and for
demonstrating such patience and
professionalism.

Tamsin Blanchard wishes to thank Philip
Somerville, Annelise Matthew at the
Chelsea Design Company, Jacques Azagury,
Jimmy Choo, Mark Doerfel, Eileen Graham
and Marilyn Inglis for their help.

Every effort has been made to ensure that
the information contained in this book is
correct. The publishers and authors regret
any omissions or inaccuracies.

The photograph on page 168 is by Peter
Lindbergh, and is used by kind permission of
Christian Dior, Paris.